BISCUIT

From classic family favourites to beautiful iced delights

Miranda Gore Browne

EBURY
PRESS

To **Edward**, for his love, devotion, encouragement and patience in understanding my immersion in the world of baking and writing. To **Thomas**, my favourite jammy dodger in the whole world and my expert taster – a harsher but more adorable judge than any other I have encountered. To **Eleanor**, who adores a bourbon but is not amused by a Squashed Fly – for her egg-breaking expertise and huge enthusiasm for baking.

10 9 8 7 6 5 4 3 2 1

Published in 2012 by Ebury Press, an imprint of Ebury Publishing

A Random House Group Company

The Random House Group Limited Reg. No. 954009

Addresses for companies within the Random House Group can be found at www.randomhouse.co.uk

A CIP catalogue record for this book is available from the British Library

The Random House Group Limited supports The Forest Stewardship Council (FSC®), the leading international forest certification organisation. Our books carrying the FSC label are printed on FSC® certified paper. FSC is the only forest certification scheme endorsed by the leading environmental organisations, including Greenpeace. Our paper procurement policy can be found at www.randomhouse.co.uk/environment

To buy books by your favourite authors and register for offers visit www.randomhouse.co.uk

Printed and bound in Germany by Appl Druck, Wemding

Design: Two Associates
Photography: Laura Edwards
Food styling: Katie Giovanni
Prop styling: Polly Webb Wilson

ISBN 9780091945022

CONTENTS

Message from Miranda

When I was growing up, baking was a key part of family life. I would often rush home from school to bake something, or call in at my grandmother's house, just around the corner, to choose a recipe from one of her old cookbooks. I spent hours baking and icing cakes, and at Christmas we always made our own puddings, mince pies and gingerbread biscuits. I loved working my way through cookbooks, trying out pastry, meringues and bread, and borrowing recipes from family and friends.

Biscuits are something I've always particularly loved baking. They bring back memories of happy times spent as a family, of parties and adventures. We always took homemade biscuits on our walks, and big tins of biscuits on holiday to munch on canal boats or outside tents. My mother made us party biscuits for our birthdays, and her mother made them for her. Biscuits are in my genes.

And I know I'm not the only one. Biscuits are a wonderful part of our heritage – perhaps even a British obsession. Everyone has an opinion about their favourites, and the mere mention of a bourbon or 'squashed fly' biscuit can trigger childhood memories and fierce debates about which are the most irresistible, and which is the best method of eating them. To dunk or not to dunk? With chocolate coating or without? Is a Jaffa Cake a cake or a biscuit?

Biscuits are wonderfully varied and versatile. They can be a treat between meals, a personalised gift, or a gesture to say you are thinking of someone. They can be exquisite and elegant (hand-iced for a wedding, a christening or a party), or they can be simple and sustaining. They can be eaten with a morning cup of coffee, wrapped in foil for nourishment on a long walk, or devoured by children when they get home from school. There is no limit to the world of biscuit-making, and in this book you will find recipes for every type of biscuit you can imagine, from my version of familiar favourites to twists on the classics, as well as new flavour combinations and ideas that I hope you will try. Several recipes I have gleaned from friends or adapted from delicious biscuits I have enjoyed when out and about, but *all* the recipes have been chosen simply because I love them.

I like to bake with friends and family around, and most of the biscuits in this book are ones you can make while chatting in the kitchen. I have tried to keep the recipes as straightforward as possible and to offer useful tips, but I have also included a few more demanding ones for very special occasions. I love to escape to the kitchen at the dead of night and decorate pretty biscuits when I can concentrate and enjoy being creative in my own world of icing and piping bags. When I made decorated biscuits on *The Great British Bake Off,* I said I felt like I was sending out little members of my family to be judged, and I still believe that. A bit of love goes into every biscuit I make, and I grow attached to each and every one. I think even the simplest biscuit can look stunning when it is homemade, simply because it shows you care.

I've written the recipes for those attempting their first forays into biscuit baking, as well as for more confident bakers. I hope that making biscuits will become something that you love to do, and that these recipes will become family favourites or adored by friends because they remind them of you.

Happy biscuit baking!

Love

Miranda x

Introduction

Like any skill, baking has certain requirements to ensure a successful end product. This section outlines what you need to make the best biscuits in the world.

Ingredients

I firmly believe that it is essential to use really good-quality ingredients. You are going to put a great deal of love and attention into making your biscuits, so it makes sense to put the same care into choosing your ingredients. Most of the recipes need just simple and inexpensive basics, but the ratios vary and the ingredients are combined in different ways to make a huge variety of textures, from crumbly shortbread to crunchy cantucci.

BUTTER

Always use unsalted butter, and make sure it is at the temperature specified. The consistency of the butter – hard and straight from the fridge, firm but at room temperature, or softened and squidgy – makes a huge difference to the success of a recipe, so do follow the instructions given. You will find that room temperature butter is best when the recipe requires it to be chopped, and softened butter is best for creaming.

CHOCOLATE

Chocolate with a high percentage of cocoa solids (over 70%) has different properties from the dark chocolate found in sweet shops, which has more like 44% cocoa solids. The amount of cocoa solids and cocoa butter can have a marked effect on the consistency and taste of the finished recipe: biscuits might be too heavy or dry if made with chocolate of a higher cocoa content than specified, while ganache may separate or split if the chocolate does not contain enough cocoa butter. For these reasons, it is important to use the chocolate specified in the ingredients list.

Melting chocolate: The best way to melt chocolate is to place it in a heatproof bowl over a pan of simmering water, without the bottom of the bowl actually touching the water. Stir regularly, taking great care that not even a drop of water gets into the chocolate or it will become grainy.

An alternative method is to put the chocolate in a microwave-safe bowl (one that does not become hot during microwaving – this is important to prevent the chocolate continuing to be heated after removal from the oven) and microwave on Medium in 30-second blasts. Stir between each blast and keep a careful eye on it to avoid burning.

EGGS

All the recipes use large (size 2) eggs, preferably free-range or organic, unless stated otherwise. It is important to use the right size of egg otherwise your biscuit dough will be too sticky or fail to bind together.

Eggs should be kept at room temperature or taken out of the fridge at least 30 minutes before use because this makes them easier to incorporate into the flour mixture, and they whisk up to a greater volume than cold eggs.

FLAVOURINGS

When using oranges or lemons, choose organic unwaxed varieties because the zest will have a much stronger citrus taste.

When vanilla is called for, the seeds from vanilla pods give by far the best flavour, so do try to use them where specified. Vanilla extract and vanilla bean paste give a very different taste from vanilla pods and will change the colour of pale cut-out biscuits, making them browner. Both pods and extract are used in this book, so for the best results, try to use whatever is stated in the recipes.

Put used vanilla pods into a jar of caster sugar to make the most wonderful vanilla sugar. In the recipes, this can be used instead of mixing plain sugar with vanilla.

FLOUR

If you want a really fine, delicate texture to your biscuits, you can buy superfine or '00' flour. Otherwise, use the type specified in the recipe.

Note that it is not necessary to sift the flour in every recipe. This is only required when extra air in the mixture is beneficial.

NUTS

Many of the recipes in this book call for toasted nuts (whole or chopped), which are very easy to make yourself. Simply place them on a baking sheet in the oven while it is coming up to temperature and heat as follows, allowing them to cool before peeling or using.

Almonds: About 8 minutes.
Hazelnuts: About 10 minutes. Rub off the dry skin using a clean tea towel.
Pecans: About 5 minutes, but watch them carefully as they burn very easily.
Walnuts: About 5 minutes. Rub off the dry skin using a clean tea towel.

Grinding nuts: A food processor is fantastic for grinding nuts, but you can easily do this by hand. Simply put the nuts into a strong freezer bag or a large mixing bowl and bash them with the end of a rolling pin.

RAISING AGENTS

Biscuits require a number of different raising agents – bicarbonate of soda, baking powder and cream of tartar – and it is worth having all of them in your cupboard. Do not be tempted to omit them or swap one for another as this can significantly change the resulting biscuit.

SUGARS

I have often been tempted to use the sugar I have in the cupboard rather than the type a recipe specifies, but biscuits are very sensitive to different types of sugar, which can radically affect their texture and moisture. It is important to use the type of sugar specified in order to achieve a successful biscuit.

Making and Baking

Biscuits love to be looked after. If you take care and treat them well while making them, they will reward you. The best biscuits are born from a dough that has been carefully handled.

USEFUL BAKING EQUIPMENT

Biscuits can be made with minimal equipment, and household objects can be pressed into service – a bottle instead of a rolling pin, an empty tin or upturned tumbler instead of a cutter – but if you are looking to buy some useful things, you will never regret investing in the following items:

- Baking trays (two or three good-quality flat ones)
- Digital scales
- Digital timer
- Flour shaker (also useful for icing sugar)
- Measuring jug
- Measuring spoons
- Metal cutters
- Non-stick baking paper/parchment/ greaseproof paper
- Oven thermometer
- Palette knives (a large one for lifting biscuits off baking trays, and two or three small ones for mixing and spreading icing, and tidying and lifting tiny biscuits)
- Piping bags (you can buy a roll of non-stick bags)
- Piping nozzles (sizes 01 and 02, plus a large star nozzle)
- Rolling pin, non-stick
- Sieve
- Wire cooling rack

WEIGHING AND MEASURING

Try to weigh as accurately as possible. I moved to digital scales while practising for *The Great British Bake Off* and I have never looked back. Careful weighing really does deliver better baking. Measure liquids accurately using a clear measuring jug with detailed markings (stand the jug on a flat surface and check the liquid is at the correct level). If the amount of liquid is wrong, your dough will either be sticky and too soft to handle, or dry and crumbly.

Spoon measurements all refer to metric measuring spoons. Fill the spoon with the ingredient and level with a knife before adding to the recipe.

MIXERS AND FOOD PROCESSORS

For recipes that require butter and sugar to be creamed together, I recommend using a mixer as I find it gives the best results. If you don't have a mixer, simply make sure your butter is really soft and use a wooden spoon or balloon whisk to beat it furiously.

For recipes that require eggs to be whisked until stiff, use a mixer with a whisk attachment. Alternatively, use a balloon whisk (and plenty of patience and elbow grease).

For recipes that require butter to be rubbed into sugar, the quickest and best results come from using a food processor. If you don't have one, rub the ingredients together with your fingertips.

For finely grinding ingredients such as nuts, a food processor is fantastic (see page 7).

CHILLING DOUGH

Always chill dough in the fridge, wrapped tightly in cling film, unless the recipe states otherwise, and try to keep to the recommended chilling time. When making cut-out biscuits, it is helpful to give the dough a second chilling, after cutting, as this helps the biscuits to hold their shape better. Just lay them on a prepared baking tray and chill for anything from 15 minutes to 2 hours (even 5 minutes is better than nothing) before putting them in the oven.

ROLLING OUT DOUGH

Some recipes specify rolling out dough between sheets of cling film rather than using a dusting of flour. This is because the extra flour can be incorporated into the dough and change the balance of the recipe, making your biscuits tough and dry. Rolling out between cling film stops the dough sticking to the work surface and the rolling pin, but it's still important to roll it as few times as possible because over-rolling can make the biscuits tough.

FREEZING DOUGH

Lots of biscuit dough freezes well and, if wrapped tightly in cling film, can be frozen for a couple of months. Depending on thickness, allow it to defrost for about an hour or so at room temperature before using. Try to resist defrosting in the microwave as, unless you are extremely careful, the dough will start to melt in the middle.

CUTTERS

It is really useful to have some round cutters, fluted and plain, in different sizes. It is also fun to have a selection of shaped cutters – perhaps a few gingerbread men, a star, a heart and some shapes personal to you. I have an inventory of all mine, and love adding new shapes to my collection. Cutters are made in various materials, but all are inexpensive to buy. I prefer to use those made of metal or copper as they give a lovely clean shape to biscuits, but plastic cutters are fine too.

Note: In every recipe I have indicated roughly how many biscuits the mixture will make. However, that number may vary, depending on how big you make each biscuit.

BAKING TRAYS

Low-edged or completely flat baking trays are best for baking biscuits as they allow the heat to circulate properly. Always line your trays with non-stick baking paper if stated in the recipe. It is really useful to have two, or ideally three, baking trays, as this allows you to use up a whole quantity of dough in one go. If you have only one tray, remove the first batch of baked biscuits and run the tray under cold water and dry it before lining with a fresh piece of baking paper and covering it with more biscuits. Never put uncooked biscuits onto a hot baking tray as they will melt and spread before they start to bake, and lose their shape. Bake biscuits in the middle and bottom of the oven, unless the recipe says otherwise.

Try to bake similar-sized biscuits on the same tray, as different sizes take different times to cook. This is particularly important when you are making cut-out biscuits.

SPACING

Lots of biscuits spread during baking, so to ensure they don't stick together, it is important to space them about 3 cm apart. If they need even more space than this, it is stated in the recipe.

OVEN TEMPERATURES AND BAKING ADVICE

Always heat the oven to the correct temperature before starting to bake your biscuits. If the oven is not hot enough, the dough will melt before it starts to bake, which will lead to flat and unappetising biscuits. Ovens vary hugely in temperature, so it is worth investing in an oven thermometer to test the accuracy of yours (I used one for making all the recipes in this book). The thermometer is a small and inexpensive device that sits on the oven shelf and records the actual temperature – you'll be amazed how different it can be from what's shown on the external dial.

A thermometer is also very useful even if you have a gas oven because some electric oven temperatures (e.g. 170°C) do not have an exact gas equivalent – the nearest is Mark 3, the same as for 160°C. In this case, biscuits baked in a gas oven will need to bake for a little longer than specified at 170°C, but keep a constant eye on them as biscuits can go from perfect to burnt in moments.

Biscuits are fairly resilient – you can open the oven door to have a peek without spoiling them – so for the first few batches you make, it is worth checking them a little before the stated baking time is up to ensure they are not overdone. Always set a timer as biscuits bake rapidly.

AGAS AND RAYBURNS

Traditional Agas and Rayburns do not have immediate temperature regulation, so you are restricted to cooking with the temperature in the oven on the day you want to bake. Aga temperatures can be influenced by the weather outside (the temperature can drop if it is very windy or cold) and by how much you have already used the Aga that day. Given these variables, the cooking times will differ from those stated in the recipes. (For example, if the temperature is quite low, the biscuits will need a longer baking time.) Using an oven thermometer will help you to calculate more accurate baking times.

If you have a four-oven Aga, bake the biscuits in the baking oven, which has a moderate temperature. Biscuits baked in this oven should need about the same time as the recipe states but, again, this will vary, depending on the overall temperature of the Aga. It is advisable to check the biscuits before the end time stated in the recipe.

If you have a two-oven Aga, put the cold plain shelf at the top of the roasting oven. This should give you the perfect biscuit-baking temperature for at least 30 minutes. You might need to swap to another cold plain shelf if you need the oven for longer. If the biscuits are baking too fast underneath, add another cold shelf to the bottom of the oven. Check the biscuits halfway through the cooking time, and if they are browning more at the side of the tray next to the burner, rotate it through 180°C so that they bake evenly.

You might prefer to bake meringues and macaroons in the simmering oven; an oven thermometer will help you to decide whether this is a more suitable choice.

FAN OVENS

Usually about 10–20°C hotter than conventional ovens, fan ovens need to be adjusted accordingly. Ideally, check the temperature with an oven thermometer.

STORING BISCUITS

If stored properly, lots of biscuits will keep well for up to two weeks. Always store them in an airtight container, and add a few sugar cubes if you like, as this helps to keep them crisp. Never store biscuits in the same container as cakes or they will become soggy. If biscuits lose their crunch, simply freshen them up in the oven at about 140°C/Mark 1 for 5 minutes before serving.

Baked biscuits (minus filling and decoration) also freeze well provided they are placed in a sealed plastic bag or box. Defrost at room temperature, then pop them into the oven at 140°C/Mark 1 for 5 minutes to freshen them up.

Troubleshooting

There are some common fears with baking biscuits; I hope I've dispelled some of them here.

HOW DO I KNOW IF MY BISCUITS ARE BAKED?

If you are making cut-out biscuits, lift one up with a large palette knife and peek underneath. If the base is a mottled golden colour, you have a perfect bake. Other biscuits (hand-shaped or piped) should be pale golden and dryish on top. Lots of biscuits will still be quite soft at the end of the baking time, tending to harden or firm up as they cool. The key thing is not to overbake them because that cannot be rectified; undercooked biscuits can always be returned to the oven for a few more minutes.

WHAT MAKES BISCUITS SPREAD TOO MUCH?

If biscuits spread a lot during baking, this could be for several reasons: a) too much butter was added; b) the butter was not the correct consistency or temperature; c) too much liquid was added; d) the oven was not up to temperature, so the biscuits melted before baking. Double-check your measurements so you know what went wrong.

A good way of salvaging biscuits that have spread and merged is to slice them into neat pieces before serving. Alternatively, crumble them up and use as 'rubble' for rocky road (see page 20), a cheesecake base or for sprinkling on ice cream.

WHY ARE MY BISCUITS SOGGY?

Lots of biscuits are soft when they come out of the oven, but harden as they cool. If they are still soggy after cooling, this could be because: a) they have not been baked long enough; b) they have been left out in the air too long; c) they were kept in a tin that was not airtight. Bake for another 4–5 minutes at the recommended oven temperature.

WHY ARE MY BISCUITS TOO HARD?

There are three main reasons why biscuits might be too hard: a) they do not contain enough butter – check that you added the correct amount; b) too much flour was added either when making or, more probably, when rolling out; c) they have been overbaked, i.e. baked for too long, which is the most common reason for hard biscuits.

Icing and Decorating

There are many ways to decorate biscuits, and below are listed the principal ones.

BUTTERCREAM

Soft butter beaten with sifted icing sugar and flavouring (such as lemon or chocolate) makes a delicious creamy icing. It's also great for sandwiching biscuits together.

ROLL-OUT ICING

Ready-made icing is available in a huge range of colours and ideal for decorating lots of cut-out biscuits quickly. Simply roll it out to a thickness of about 3 mm, then cut out shapes with the same cutter you used to make your biscuits. Stick the icing shapes onto the biscuits with a few dabs of royal icing.

ROYAL ICING

This type of icing sets hard and can be coloured with liquid colour paste. Buy royal icing sugar and mix according to the packet instructions. Make a stiff icing to pipe writing, outlines and decorations, and a runnier icing to fill in outlines (see pages 187–188 for detailed instructions on how to do this).

SUGAR FLORIST PASTE

It is possible to buy lots of very pretty, ready-made icing decorations, but it is very easy to make your own using sugar florist paste (available from specialist cake decorating shops or online suppliers). While the paste is expensive, you need only a small amount. Roll it out very thinly, then use cutters to stamp out decorations. They will go completely hard and last for at least three months in a sealed container. Stick them onto biscuits with a dab of royal icing.

WATER ICING

Made from icing sugar mixed with water and/or lemon juice, water icing is useful for both decorating and glazing biscuits, and can be mixed with food colouring. If making children's biscuits, the icing can be flavoured and lightly coloured with fruit spreads (see page 154). It will harden a little, but should not go completely hard.

If you want icing recipes and further information about colouring and decorating, see pages 184–189.

USEFUL DECORATING EQUIPMENT

- Cocktail sticks (for making indented patterns, for detailed icing and decorating)
- Icing bottles (great for children to decorate with – available from cake decorating shops and Lakeland)
- Icing cutters (smaller than pastry cutters, and specifically for icing)
- Liquid colour paste
- Non-stick piping bags
- Piping nozzles (01 for writing, 02 for borders and 1 cm star or flower nozzles for piping buttercream)
- Small lidded plastic pots (to store icing)

Baking with children

I baked a great deal as a child, and the thing I remember most about it is licking the mixing bowl at the end. It's the reason children love to bake, and I think it's important that they get a chance to enjoy the bits they value as well as all the bits we want them to enjoy.

There is plenty of learning in baking, but you don't really need to draw attention to it. Unconsciously, children will learn a huge amount about science, and they will become very good at weighing and measuring. Older children will love reading recipes and giving instructions. Having a pen at the ready to tick off a list of all the ingredients as they are added is a great discipline for future bakers.

If you are baking with more than one child, allocating tasks always seems to lead to a more relaxed atmosphere. Taking it in turns to use the equipment and do the things a small child deems most important are usually key to a quiet and contented baking experience. In our kitchen, control of the mixer is generally in the competent hands of my seven-year-old son, Thomas, which suits my four-year-old daughter, Eleanor, just fine because she believes the digital scales are the command centre of operations.

We have basic rules, such as that hands must be washed and aprons worn at all times. Consumption of ingredients throughout the baking process is permitted because I think it is really important for children to understand how raw ingredients taste and for them to try new things. However, I do encourage them to ask before they eat, otherwise measurements tend to go haywire.

Make sure you have enough time. Baking with children always takes longer than planned, and there is nothing more likely to induce stress than trying to rush things. Also, avoid tackling ambitious projects, at least to start with. Everyone thrives and gains confidence from doing simple things well and achieving a delicious end result.

Children bake better if they are baking things they want to eat. Encourage them to try out different recipes and make it exciting, but try not to get frustrated if they want to repeat the same recipe quite a few times. It will probably become their signature bake for life, and there is nothing wrong with any of us having a memorised favourite recipe up our sleeve.

Try not to underestimate children's ability, and let them have a go at difficult parts of the process. Even the youngest children can be good at the trickiest things (I was most surprised to discover that my daughter at two years old was able to fill my icing bottles).

I know from experience that if I stay relaxed, we all enjoy baking more. Mess can always be cleaned up, and we usually have a massive tidy-up time together when everything is cooking in the oven.

The most important rule is to have fun and remember that you are doing something very valuable indeed – you are creating the next generation of bakers.

1 BISCUITS FOR BEGINNERS

Making biscuits is a great introduction to baking, but I hope everyone will enjoy these recipes, regardless of experience. Whether you are a complete beginner, keen to get baking with your children or grandchildren, or just hanker to make something delicious and homemade, this chapter is the place to start.

I like to know what my children are eating and look in horror at the ingredients lists on packets of shop-bought biscuits. Although some of the biscuits in this chapter are indulgent and studded with sweeties, others are crammed with healthy oats and fruit. The great thing about all of them is that you know what they contain. I often make them with organic ingredients to make them even better for little ones.

The recipes that follow are really easy to make and use ingredients you will usually have to hand in your kitchen. (I have also included some of my favourite variations so that even if you are running low on supplies, you should be able to make most of them.) I hope you will come back to them again and again and use them as the basis for making your own variations. As I am passionate about getting children baking, I would like these recipes to show just how much fun baking biscuits can be. From my own experience, I am confident these recipes will get children hooked and wanting to bake more and more.

Each recipe will easily fill a biscuit tin, but I am pretty sure the results of your efforts will be devoured from the cooling rack while still warm. Even the simplest, homemade biscuits taste so much better than anything you can buy in the shops.

Rusks for rascals

Perfect for rascals of all ages, these biscuits look rather like a rustic version of biscotti. They store well and are great for dunking in milk, hot chocolate or a creamy cappuccino, so keep a tinful on standby.

MAKES ABOUT 40

125 g unsalted butter, at room temperature, plus extra for greasing and dotting

375 g plain flour

100 g demerara sugar

125 g caster sugar

½ tsp salt

1 tsp baking powder

200 ml semi-skimmed milk

1 tbsp vinegar

icing sugar, to dust

Tip: If more convenient, switch the oven off and leave the slices to dry inside it for a couple of hours, or overnight if you prefer.

Chop the butter and rub it into the flour with your fingertips or whizz in a food processor. Add the sugars, salt and baking powder and stir to combine.

Put the milk and vinegar in a jug; it will curdle, so this is a great recipe to use up old milk that is past its best. Add the liquid to the dry mixture a little at a time, stirring after each addition, until it comes together as a dough. It will be very sticky.

Preheat the oven to 190°C/Mark 5. Choose a large baking tray, the biggest you have, and grease liberally with butter. Dust with flour and keep close at hand.

With wet hands to prevent the dough sticking to them, divide it in half and roll into two rough logs. Place them side by side on the baking tray but with as much of a gap as possible between them. Don't worry if they look messy – they are meant to at this stage. Dot about 6 tablespoons of butter on the tray and bake for 45 minutes, or until the tops of the logs are golden and crusty. Remove from the oven and reduce the temperature to 150°C/Mark 2.

Leave the logs, now joined in the middle, to cool for about 5 minutes. Transfer them to a chopping board and cut to separate, then use a large knife to slice them into about 20 pieces roughly 2 cm wide. Allow the slices to cool, then break each of them in half with your hands. Spread them out on the baking tray and return to the oven for 30 minutes. Turn the slices over and bake for a further 30 minutes. Set aside to cool completely, and dust with icing sugar before serving.

Fabulous fork biscuits

In this recipe, two flavours of biscuit are made in moments from the same basic dough. In fact, you could make them while chatting to a friend and be eating them before the conversation is over. Raspberry and chocolate are my favourite flavours, but you can add whatever you like to these fabulous biscuits.

MAKES ABOUT 12 OF
EACH FLAVOUR
250 g unsalted butter,
softened
125 g caster sugar

FOR RASPBERRY
BISCUITS
50 g fresh raspberries,
unwashed
150 g self-raising flour

FOR CHOCOLATE
BISCUITS
125 g self-raising flour
15 g cocoa powder

Cream the butter and sugar, then spoon half of the mixture into a separate bowl.

To one of the bowls add the raspberries and beat furiously to combine. Add the flour and stir thoroughly.

Sift the flour and cocoa powder into the other bowl and mix well. In both cases, the dough will be quite wet.

Preheat the oven to 180°C/Mark 4 and line two baking trays with non-stick baking paper.

Using either floured hands, a small ice-cream scoop or 2 tablespoons, make 12 walnut-sized balls of dough from each bowl of mixture and place them on separate prepared trays, spacing them at least 3 cm apart. Use a fork to flatten them slightly, dipping it in cold water before pressing it on each ball so that it leaves a clean indent and doesn't stick.

Bake for 10–15 minutes, or until the biscuits are dry and firm on top. Leave to cool on the trays for at least 5 minutes, then use a palette knife to transfer them carefully to a wire rack to cool completely.

Fruity little teds

Easy and inexpensive to make, these buttery biscuits are eggless, packed with fruit and free of 'nasties', so they are great for toddlers, but older children and grown-ups will love them too. It is important not to wash the strawberries as they soak up too much liquid and will make the dough wet and sticky.

MAKES AT LEAST 12

100 g fresh strawberries, unwashed, or 100 g ripe banana

100 g unsalted butter, softened

100 g golden caster sugar

200 g plain flour

YOU WILL ALSO NEED

Teddy-shaped metal cutter (optional)

Use a piece of kitchen paper to brush the strawberries clean, then hull them. Press through a sieve using the back of a spoon, and keep pressing until only the seeds remain. If using banana, mash it with a fork.

Cream the butter and sugar, adding the banana (if using) at the same time: the mixture becomes lovely and smooth.

Add the puréed strawberries to the creamed mixture and stir well, adding a spoonful of flour if it seems to curdle. Add the remaining flour and mix well. The dough will be very sticky but the stickiness will disappear after chilling. Wrap it in cling film and pop in the fridge for at least 1 hour.

Preheat the oven to 180°C/Mark 4 and line two baking trays with non-stick baking paper.

Place the chilled dough between two sheets of cling film and roll out to a thickness of about 5 mm. Use a teddy-shaped metal cutter to stamp out shapes. Alternatively, roll the dough into walnut-sized balls. Place the shapes or balls on the prepared trays, spacing them at least 3 cm apart. Squash the balls flat with a wet fork.

Bake for 15–20 minutes, or until the biscuits are golden brown around the edges. Allow to cool on their trays for 10 minutes, then use a palette knife to transfer them carefully to a wire rack and leave until completely cold.

Rocky road

I have adapted this recipe over the years and now I think it is just right. It's great for making with children as it is very forgiving of any measuring mistakes and doesn't involve an oven. You can add whatever ingredients you have in the cupboard, such as chopped apricots, rice crispies, coconut and chopped-up chocolate bars. If you are making this for children, for a special treat you can increase the milk chocolate or add white chocolate chunks. If serving to grown-ups as an after-dinner treat, cut into smaller pieces and use just dark chocolate with a higher cocoa content.

MAKES AT LEAST 16

350 g good-quality chocolate (200 g dark chocolate [70% cocoa solids] and 150 g milk chocolate [30% cocoa solids] works really well)

150 g unsalted butter

4 tbsp golden syrup

175 g Rich Tea biscuits

150 g raisins or sultanas

200 g glacé cherries, halved or roughly chopped

2 handfuls mini marshmallows

icing sugar, to dust

Put the chocolate, butter and syrup in a large pan and melt gently over a low heat – do not allow it to boil. Once melted, set aside.

Put the Rich Tea biscuits in a large mixing bowl and crush them with the end of a rolling pin, leaving some large chunks. Add the raisins and glacé cherries to the crushed biscuits, then pour in the syrup mixture and stir well until everything is evenly covered.

Line a brownie tin with cling film – this prevents the rocky road sticking and saves on washing up too. Sprinkle half the marshmallows into the prepared tin, then cover with the chocolate biscuit mixture. Sprinkle over the rest of the marshmallows, squash the mixture into the edges of the tin and press down quite firmly with a palette knife. Chill for at least 2–3 hours, or ideally overnight if you can wait that long.

Once completely firm, lift out the slab of rocky road by using the cling film and put right-side up on a chopping board. Cut into squares or fingers and dust generously with icing sugar before serving.

* Miranda's Variations

If you're feeling really indulgent, cover the top of the chilled slab of rocky road with a thin layer of melted chocolate (about 150 g) and allow to set in the fridge for at least another hour before slicing into pieces.

Imagination biscuits

These biscuits can truly be anything you want them to be. Melting, buttery and delicious just as they are, they are great fun to decorate too. Let children's imagination run wild with the shapes and decoration, making spaceships, monsters, zoo animals ... whatever they like.

MAKES AT LEAST 24

200 g unsalted butter, softened

200 g caster sugar

½ tsp vanilla extract or grated zest of ½ an orange or lemon

1 medium egg, lightly beaten

375 g plain flour or 350 g plain flour and 25 g cocoa powder

royal icing or water icing in various colours (see Tips, page 13), or 50 g melted chocolate (see page 6), for decoration

YOU WILL ALSO NEED

Medium cutters (whatever shape you desire)

Icing bottles (see page 13) or piping bags

Cream the butter and sugar with the vanilla or zest. Add the egg a little at a time, mixing well after each addition. Mix in the flour (or flour and cocoa), on a low speed if using a mixer, until a dough forms. Bring it together with your hands, then shape into two flat discs. Wrap each of them tightly in cling film and chill for at least 30 minutes.

Preheat the oven to 180°C/Mark 4 and line two baking trays with non-stick baking paper.

Roll out each piece of chilled dough between two sheets of cling film to a thickness of 3–5 mm. Cut into your chosen shapes and place on the prepared trays, spacing them at least 3 cm apart. If you have time, chill for 15 minutes as this will help the biscuits to hold their shape in the oven.

Bake for about 10 minutes, until the biscuits are golden brown at the edges and the base is mottled and golden. Allow to cool on the trays for 2–3 minutes, then use a palette knife to transfer them carefully to a wire rack.

When the biscuits are completely cold, fill icing bottles or piping bags with various colours of royal icing or water icing and use to decorate the biscuits. (Children find icing bottles much easier to use.) Alternatively, use melted chocolate to stick on decorations, such as small sweets or sprinkles.

Coconut jammy thumbprints

You will have great fun with these biscuits, and little hands will have lots of jobs to keep them busy. They're perfect for baking on a rainy day, and for munching together.

MAKES AT LEAST 24

225 g unsalted butter, softened

225 g caster sugar

½ tsp vanilla extract

1 egg plus 1 egg yolk, lightly beaten

200 g plain flour

125 g desiccated coconut

strawberry jam

Preheat the oven to 180°C/Mark 4 and line two baking trays with non-stick baking paper.

Cream the butter, sugar and vanilla extract until light and fluffy. Add the eggs a little at a time, beating well after each addition. Sift the flour into the mixture and add 75 g of the desiccated coconut. Mix well until a sticky dough forms.

Put the remaining 50 g coconut onto a large plate. Take teaspoonfuls of the dough and roll in the coconut, handling the balls as little as possible so that the dough does not start to melt from the warmth of your hands. If it gets too warm and is very sticky, pop it in the fridge to cool down a bit.

Place the balls on the prepared trays, spacing them at least 5 cm apart. Put some flour in a cup and get the children to dip their thumbs in it before making a thumbprint in the middle of each biscuit – they'll love doing this, but make sure they dip in the flour each time or you'll end up with a sticky mess.

When all the balls of dough have dents in the middle, fill them with jam. I think strawberry jam works best with the coconut, but feel free to use another flavour, or experiment with chocolate spread.

Bake for 15–20 minutes, or until pale golden and dry on top. (If you don't have enough space in the oven for all your biscuits, pop the waiting biscuits in the fridge until it is their turn to be baked.) The biscuits are very floppy when they come out of the oven, so leave them on their trays until they are completely cold and firm.

Twirly-whirly biscuits

... or snail biscuits, as my children Thomas and Eleanor love to call them.

MAKES AT LEAST 24

250 g plain flour

¼ tsp salt

¼ tsp baking powder

100 g caster sugar

225 g unsalted butter,
    at room temperature,
    roughly chopped

1 tsp vanilla extract

25 g cocoa powder, sifted

1 egg white, lightly
    beaten

YOU WILL ALSO NEED

Pastry brush

Miranda's Variations

Add a thin layer of hazelnut chocolate spread between the layers of dough and sprinkle it with finely chopped hazelnuts before rolling up.

Sift all the dry ingredients (except the cocoa powder) into a bowl. Add the butter, then rub together with your fingertips or whizz in a food processor until the mixture resembles coarse breadcrumbs.

Place roughly half the mixture on a work surface, sprinkle with the vanilla and knead gently to combine. Squash into a flat disc, then wrap tightly in cling film and chill for at least 1 hour.

Add the cocoa powder to the mixture left in the bowl and stir or whizz until a dough forms. Squash into a flat disc, then wrap tightly in cling film and chill for at least 1 hour.

Place the chilled vanilla dough between two sheets of cling film and roll into a rectangle about 1 cm thick. Do exactly the same with the chocolate dough.

Carefully remove the dough from the cling film. Brush one rectangle with the egg white. Lay the other rectangle on top (it doesn't matter if they are not exactly the same size). Place the double layer of dough between two fresh sheets of cling film and roll into a rectangle about 5 mm thick.

Remove the top sheet of cling film and roll the dough up from the longest side, using the bottom sheet of cling film to help you and smoothing the dough together as you roll. You should end up with a long log about 3–4 cm in diameter. Cut it in half and wrap each piece in cling film. Chill for at least 1 hour).

Preheat the oven to 180°C/Mark 4 and line two baking trays with non-stick baking paper.

Cut the dough into 5 mm slices. Place on a lined baking tray, spacing them at least 3 cm apart, and bake for 10–15 minutes, or until turning golden around the edges. Leave the biscuits to cool on their trays for about 5 minutes, then use a palette knife to transfer them to a wire rack to cool completely.

Blueberry bumbles

These are simple, crunchy biscuits, and their combination of grated orange zest, blueberries and white chocolate is yummy.

MAKES AT LEAST 24

125 g unsalted butter, softened

100 g soft light brown sugar

grated zest of ½ an orange

1 egg, beaten

225 g plain flour

¼ tsp baking powder

50 g dried blueberries

50 g white chocolate chips

Cream the butter and sugar with the orange zest until light and fluffy. Mix in the beaten egg a little at a time until well combined. Fold in the flour and baking powder using a metal spoon, and mix until a dough starts to form. Add the blueberries and chocolate chips and mix until combined.

Tip the dough onto a lightly floured surface and knead gently for about 20 seconds. Roll into two log shapes about 6 cm in diameter, then wrap each one in cling film and put in the fridge for at least 1 hour. (If you wish, the dough could be frozen at this point for future use. Defrost at room temperature for about 1 hour, then slice and bake as described below.)

Preheat the oven to 200ºC/ Mark 6 and line a baking tray with non-stick baking paper.

Cut each chilled log into 12 slices (about 1 cm thick) and place on the prepared tray. Bake for 8–10 minutes, or until pale golden. Leave the biscuits to cool on their trays for at least 5 minutes, then use a palette knife to transfer them carefully to a wire rack.

Sweetie biscuits

Studded with colourful sweets, these biscuits are so big that you'll need two hands to eat them. If you're under 10, they are probably the kind of biscuits you dream of. My son Thomas loves me to make them when his friends come to play.

MAKES ABOUT 12

225 g unsalted butter, softened

175 g caster sugar

100 g light muscovado sugar

2 eggs, beaten

1 tsp vanilla extract

300 g self-raising flour

175 g Smarties or chocolate buttons

YOU WILL ALSO NEED

Small ice-cream scoop (optional)

Preheat the oven to 180°C/Mark 4 and line two baking trays with non-stick baking paper.

Cream the butter with both the sugars until pale and fluffy. Mix in the beaten eggs a little at a time, followed by the vanilla, until well combined. Fold in the flour using a large metal spoon.

Using a small ice-cream scoop or two tablespoons, put six dollops of the mixture on each tray, spacing them at least 3 cm apart. Bake for 8–10 minutes then remove from the oven.

While the biscuits are still on the hot baking trays, carefully press the sweets into the top of each one (it's probably best for a grown-up to do this bit). Return to the oven for a further 3–4 minutes. Leave to cool and set.

Jammy dodgers

Colourful, cheery and fun, these biscuits bring a smile to everyone's face. While impressive to look at, they are easy to make and the central hole can be cut in different shapes, such as hearts, flowers or even initials, to personalise your biscuits.

MAKES ABOUT 12

200 g unsalted butter, softened

100 g golden caster sugar

1 tsp vanilla extract

1 egg, lightly beaten

300 g plain flour, or
250 g plain flour plus
50 g ground almonds
(the nuts help the
biscuits to keep better)

about 6 tbsp good-quality
jam (strawberry and
raspberry look striking
against the pale golden
biscuits)

icing sugar, to dust

YOU WILL ALSO NEED

5 cm and 3 cm round
metal cutters, or a
tumbler and bottle cap
of the sizes suggested
(you need at least 1 cm
of biscuit around the
central hole)

Cream the butter, sugar and vanilla. Add the egg a little at a time, beating well after each addition, and scraping down the sides of the bowl to ensure everything is properly combined.

Sift the flour and ground almonds (if using) into the mixture. Mix well, but stop as soon as a dough starts to form because overmixing can make the biscuits tough. Bring the dough together with your hands, divide in half and flatten each piece into a large disc about 1 cm thick. Wrap each disc tightly in cling film and chill for at least 1 hour.

Preheat the oven to 180°C/Mark 4 and line two baking trays with non-stick baking paper.

Place the chilled dough between two sheets of cling film and roll out to a thickness of 3–4 mm. Using the large cutter, stamp out 24 circles of dough. Use the smaller cutter to stamp out a central hole in half of them.

Place the circles on the prepared trays, spacing them at least 3 cm apart. Bake for about 15 minutes, until lightly golden and mottled underneath. Allow the biscuits to cool on their trays for about 10 minutes, then use a palette knife to transfer them carefully to a wire rack. They will harden as they cool.

When they are completely cold, sandwich them together with jam – about 1 generous teaspoon per biscuit. Ideally, leave them for a day after making so the biscuits have time to stick properly and absorb some gooeyness from the jam. This is particularly important if you are giving them as a present, otherwise they will slide apart.

Chocolate toffee melts

Children love rolling balls of this chocolatey dough and pressing Rolos into them. I hardly need tell you that these are best eaten soon after baking, when the toffee is still warm and stretchy. Children adore them and grown-ups can't resist stealing them.

MAKES AT LEAST 24

225 g unsalted butter,
    softened

225 g caster sugar

2 egg yolks

2 tbsp milk

250 g plain flour

30 g cocoa powder

2 x 52 g packets of Rolos
    or chocolate-covered
    toffees

Cream the butter and sugar. Put the egg yolks in a cup, beat lightly and add to the butter mixture a little at a time, stirring until well combined. Put the milk into the eggy cup, rinse around and add to the mixture, stirring again.

Sift in the flour and cocoa powder and stir well, until a dough starts to form – this is easiest in a food mixer. Alternatively, bring the dough together with your hands and keep kneading until it forms a ball and comes away from the sides of the bowl. Ideally, wrap in cling film and chill for 30 minutes, but if you're in a hurry, move straight on to the next step.

Preheat the oven to 180°C/Mark 4 and line two baking trays with non-stick baking paper.

Using your hands, shape the dough into walnut-sized balls and place them on the prepared trays, spacing them at least 4 cm apart as they will double in size. Push a Rolo into the middle of each ball and flatten them a little with your palm. Bake for 12–15 minutes, until the biscuits look dry on top and a little cracked. Cool on their trays for about 5 minutes, then use a palette knife to transfer them carefully to a wire rack and leave until firm to the touch.

Gingerbread men

This recipe is ideal for making with children because there's no grappling with hot sugar and the mixture can all be made in one bowl. It is also very forgiving of haphazard measuring, as robust testing in many school baking classes and toddler groups has shown.

MAKES ABOUT 16

75 g unsalted butter, softened

150 g soft light brown sugar

350 g plain flour

1 tsp bicarbonate of soda

2 tsp ground ginger

4 tbsp golden syrup or honey

1 egg, beaten

2 tbsp freshly squeezed orange juice

currants, raisins or Smarties, to decorate

YOU WILL ALSO NEED

gingerbread man-shaped metal cutter

Cream the butter and the sugar. Add the flour, bicarbonate of soda and ginger and stir well.

Measure the golden syrup or honey into a small microwaveable bowl and warm in the microwave until runny. Combine with the beaten egg, then add to the flour mixture and mix well.

Mix in the orange juice a little at a time until a dough forms. Shape it into a flat disc, wrap tightly in cling film and chill for anywhere from 30 minutes to 3 days. If you like, the dough can be frozen at this point for future use. It will need about 3 hours to defrost at room temperature before you can roll it out.

Preheat the oven to 180°C/Mark 4 and line two baking trays with non-stick baking paper.

Roll out the dough on a lightly floured work surface and stamp out gingerbread men. Place them on the prepared trays, spacing them at least 3 cm apart, and chill for at least another 15 minutes.

Decorate the gingerbread men with currants, raisins or Smarties before baking if you like an old-fashioned caramelised taste, or press them in as soon as the biscuits come out of the oven. Alternatively, wait until the biscuits are completely cold and stick the decorations on with a tiny bit of melted chocolate or icing.

Bake for about 15 minutes, or until the biscuits are dry on top and slightly darker than when they went in the oven. Allow to cool on their trays for about 10 minutes, then use a palette knife to transfer them carefully to a wire rack. They will harden as they cool.

Bedtime biscuits

What could be lovelier than an oaty biscuit with a glass of milk or cup of hot chocolate last thing at night? A perfect cure for still-hungry tummies at bedtime.

MAKES AT LEAST 16

125 g unsalted butter, softened

100 g soft light brown sugar

50 g caster sugar

100 g Horlicks Original

175 g plain flour

25 g fine porridge oats

¼ tsp bicarbonate of soda

150 g sultanas

3 tbsp semi-skimmed milk

Preheat the oven to 180°C/Mark 4 and line two baking trays with non-stick baking paper.

Cream the butter and sugars. Add the Horlicks, flour, oats and bicarbonate of soda and mix well. Stir in the sultanas, then add the milk, a little at a time, until a dough starts to form. Use your hands to bring it gently together.

Roll the dough into golf ball-sized pieces and place on the prepared trays, spacing them at least 3 cm apart. Squash them flat with the palm of your hand and bake for about 12 minutes, until golden though still quite soft. Leave the biscuits on their trays to firm up for about 10 minutes, then use a palette knife to transfer them carefully to a wire rack to cool completely.

Tip: These biscuits are at their best the day you make them, so if you are not going to get through a whole batch immediately, keep half the dough in the fridge or freezer for another day

2 CUP OF TEA AND A CHAT BISCUITS

The biscuits in this chapter are for sharing with friends, for nibbling and dunking as you discuss the important issues and dramas of life over a cup of tea or coffee. These are biscuits for every day of the week.

Everyone has a favourite biscuit and the British love nothing better than comparing notes and reminiscing about their childhood favourites. Whichever biscuit you choose, you'll probably find it in this chapter, which includes many of the great everyday classics. From chocolate bourbons and custard creams to digestives and 'squashed fly' biscuits, you can wallow in retro enjoyment. I hope you love them as much as I do and that traditionalists will forgive me for capturing the spirit rather than the letter of the originals.

If you make these biscuits regular companions in your kitchen and biscuit tin, I'm sure they will help you derive even more pleasure from your cup of tea and a chat.

Chocolate bourbons

Intensely chocolatey and hugely addictive, these biscuits look gorgeously retro and have a nostalgic taste about them. I have friends who beg me to make bourbons, and I'm sure you will be inundated with requests too. Make lots and store them in the freezer. These are biscuits to impress.

MAKES ABOUT 16

110 g unsalted butter, softened

110 g soft light brown sugar

200 g plain flour

1 tsp bicarbonate of soda

40 g cocoa powder

pinch of salt

2½ tbsp golden syrup

granulated sugar, for sprinkling

Cream the butter and brown sugar. In a separate bowl, sift the flour, bicarbonate of soda, cocoa powder and salt. Add these sifted ingredients and the syrup to the butter mixture and combine until a dough forms. Bring it together with your hands, then divide it into four equal pieces. Roll each piece into a long sausage shape about 2.5 cm in diameter.

Preheat the oven to 170°C/Mark 3 and line two baking trays with non-stick baking paper.

Place a sausage of dough between two sheets of cling film (I prefer not to use flour because it marks the surface of the biscuits) and roll out to about 3 mm thick. Chill in the fridge whilst you repeat this process with the remaining dough.

Transfer the chilled pastry to a chopping board and use a pizza wheel or sharp knife to straighten the edges. When you have a neat shape, slice each piece into eight 'fingers'. Traditional bourbon biscuits measure 6 x 3 cm, so if you want to create the

FOR THE FILLING

150 g icing sugar

5 tsp cocoa powder

75 g unsalted butter,
  softened

½ tsp vanilla extract

3 tsp boiling water

YOU WILL ALSO NEED

Pizza wheel (optional)

perfect size, cut the fingers slightly smaller than this as they spread a little in the oven.

Using a palette knife, lift the biscuits onto the prepared trays, spacing them at least 2 cm apart. Now use a fine skewer to make shallow holes along the top of each biscuit – two rows of five if you're a bourbon perfectionist.

Bake for 10 minutes, until the biscuits look dry on top, then carefully check one with a palette knife. Sprinkle with granulated sugar and press it in gently with the back of a spoon. If ready, it will be fragile but should lift cleanly and neatly away from the lining paper. If not, bake for a few more minutes, then check again. When the biscuits are done, leave them on the trays for about 15 minutes, then use a palette knife to transfer them carefully to a wire rack. They will harden as they cool.

To make the filling, sift the icing sugar and cocoa into a bowl. (It is so tempting to miss out this step, but sifting is essential if you want a smooth buttercream.) Add the butter, vanilla and boiling water and beat well with a fork or hand mixer until smooth and creamy. Keep the buttercream at room temperature until you are ready to fill the biscuits.

When the biscuits are completely cold, use a palette knife to spread the filling onto the underside side of one biscuit and gently press another biscuit on top. Sandwich all the biscuits in this way.

The completed biscuits freeze brilliantly, so why not have a secret stockpile ready to impress unexpected guests who call by for a cup of tea and a chat?

Coffee and walnut biscuits

If you like coffee and walnut cake, this is the biscuit you have been waiting for. My mother and mother-in-law are obsessed with coffee and walnut cake and I often make them these biscuits if I don't have time to make a cake.

MAKES ABOUT 16

120 g unsalted butter, softened

100 g light brown muscovado sugar

1 egg, gently beaten

1½ tsp Camp coffee essence or 1 tsp instant coffee mixed with 1 tsp boiling water

125 g plain flour, sifted

pinch of salt

100 g walnuts, roughly chopped

about 16 walnut halves, to decorate

Preheat the oven to 180°C/Mark 4 and line two baking trays with non-stick baking paper.

Cream together the butter and sugar. Add the egg a little at a time, beating between each addition. Add the coffee and stir again. Finally, stir in the flour, salt and walnuts.

Using a teaspoon, place dollops of the mixture on the prepared trays, spacing them at least 3 cm apart. Press a walnut half into the top of each dollop and bake for about 15 minutes, until the biscuits look dry on top. Set aside to firm up on their trays for about 15 minutes, then use a palette knife to transfer them carefully to a wire rack. They will harden as they cool.

✳ Miranda's Variations

Why not make tiny versions for after-dinner biscuits? Replace the coffee essence with espresso and press a chocolate coffee bean on top of each biscuit as soon as it comes out of the oven.

Double chocolate chunk cookies

Chocolate biscuits with lots of chunky chocolate bits are my idea of heaven. These speak for themselves.

MAKES ABOUT 40

225 g unsalted butter, softened

250 g soft light brown sugar

100 g caster sugar

1 tsp vanilla extract

2 large eggs, gently beaten

350 g plain flour, sifted

50 g good-quality cocoa powder

½ tsp salt

2 tsp bicarbonate of soda

200 g dark chocolate chunks or chips

YOU WILL ALSO NEED

Small ice-cream scoop (optional)

Preheat the oven to 170°C/Mark 3 and line two baking trays with non-stick baking paper.

Cream together the butter, sugars and vanilla until light and fluffy. Add the eggs a little at a time, beating between each addition and scraping down the sides of the bowl to ensure everything is properly combined. Sift in the flour, cocoa, salt and bicarbonate of soda and mix until it comes together as a dough. Finally, stir in the chocolate chunks with a wooden spoon.

The dough can be frozen at this point for future use. Simply roll it into a log, wrap tightly in cling film and then baking paper tied at the ends like a Christmas cracker. When needed, defrost the dough for about 2 hours and, while still quite firm, use a sharp knife to cut into slices about 1 cm thick. Bake as below.

If using the dough straight away, take a small ice-cream scoop or two tablespoons and place walnut-sized balls of the mixture on the prepared trays, spacing them at least 3 cm apart. (If you prefer, you can roll the mixture into balls using floured hands.)

Bake for 10 minutes – the biscuits should look dry on top but will not be completely firm. Leave to cool on their trays for at least 5 minutes, then use a palette knife to transfer them carefully to a wire rack. They will harden as they cool.

✳ Miranda's Variations

Replace the cocoa with cornflour to make a traditional chocolate chip cookie.

Bakewell biscuits

These chewy, almondy biscuits are packed full of cherries, sprinkled with toasted flaked almonds and finished with gorgeous almond icing. My mother always included cherries in her version of Bakewell tart, and it is her recipe that inspired my biscuits.

MAKES ABOUT 16

125 g unsalted butter, softened

250 g caster sugar

125 g soft light brown sugar

½–1 tsp almond extract

1 egg, lightly beaten

150 g self-raising flour, preferably sifted

125 g ground almonds

175 g chopped glacé cherries

50 g flaked almonds, toasted (see page 7)

FOR THE ICING

100 g icing sugar

¼ tsp almond extract mixed with a little water

Preheat the oven to 150°C/Mark 2 and line two baking trays with non-stick baking paper.

Cream together the butter, sugars and almond extract, scraping down the sides of the bowl to ensure everything is combined. Beat in the egg. Now add the flour, ground almonds and glacé cherries and mix until a soft dough forms.

With floured hands, roll the sticky dough into balls the size of a golf ball and place on the prepared trays, spacing them at least 2 cm apart. Gently press the dough to flatten it a little, then sprinkle generously with the flaked almonds. Bake for 30–35 minutes, until puffy and pale golden. Set aside to cool on their trays for at least 5 minutes, then use a palette knife to transfer them carefully to a wire rack. Leave until completely cold. Put a sheet of greaseproof or baking paper under the rack before doing the next step.

To make the icing, mix the sugar with the almond extract and water: the mixture should be just runny enough for drizzling. I like to put it into a piping bag, snip off the corner to make a tiny hole, then make zigzag lines to give a pretty finish. Leave the icing to set a little before eating.

Tip: Make smaller biscuits and sandwich them together with raspberry jam to enhance the heavenly Bakewell experience.

Jam roly-poly biscuits

Soft, buttery vanilla biscuits rolled with jam and sprinkled with sugar – these are comfort food at its best. Red jam, such as strawberry or raspberry, makes a stunning contrast to the vanilla biscuit.

MAKES ABOUT 18

250 g plain flour

½ tsp baking powder

125 g caster sugar

125 g unsalted butter,
    at room temperature

seeds from 1 vanilla pod
    or 1 tsp good-quality
    vanilla extract

1 egg plus 1 egg yolk,
    lightly whisked

about 8 tbsp good-
    quality strawberry or
    raspberry jam

Sift the flour and baking powder into a bowl, add the sugar and mix to combine. Roughly chop the butter and rub it into the dry ingredients with your fingertips (or whizz in a food processor) until the mixture resembles breadcrumbs. Add the vanilla seeds or extract. With the mixer running slowly, add the whisked egg a little at a time until a dough starts to form. Tip onto a baking tray lined with baking paper and knead gently for about a minute to bring the dough together. Shape into a rough rectangle, then cover with cling film and chill for at least 1 hour.

Turn the chilled dough onto a sheet of cling film and roll out to thickness of about 5 mm, trying to keep it roughly rectangular. Spread generously with jam, then gently roll up from the long side, using the cling film to help you. Cut the log in half, wrap each piece in cling film and chill again for at least another hour.

Preheat the oven to 180°C/Mark 4 and line two baking trays with non-stick baking paper.

Unwrap the chilled logs and cut into slices no thicker than 1 cm. Place them on the prepared trays, spacing them at least 2 cm apart, and bake for 10–15 minutes, until starting to become golden. Remove from the oven and sprinkle with caster sugar. Leave to cool on their trays.

Dark chocolate digestives

One of my greatest pleasures in life is dunking plain chocolate digestives into a mug of tea. Ideally, I would also be alone, with a good book, but these biscuits have also been my companions through late nights of revision, long days with crying babies and hours of putting the world to rights with friends.

MAKES AT LEAST 16

250 g plain wholemeal flour

50 g oatmeal or rolled oats

40 g wheatgerm

½ tsp bicarbonate of soda

½ tsp salt

50 g soft light brown sugar

125 g unsalted butter, straight from the fridge

5 tbsp semi-skimmed milk

100 g dark chocolate, at least 70% cocoa solids

YOU WILL ALSO NEED

4 cm round metal cutter, or a shape of similar size

Cocktail stick or fine skewer

Preheat the oven to 180°C/Mark 4 and line two baking trays with non-stick baking paper.

Put the flour, oatmeal, wheatgerm, bicarbonate of soda, salt and sugar into a bowl and mix well.

Grate the cold butter into the bowl of dry ingredients. Combine thoroughly, using your fingertips (or whizz in a food processor) until the mixture resembles breadcrumbs. Add the milk a little at a time, mixing between each addition, until a dough forms (you can add a little more milk than specified if the mixture seems very crumbly).

Divide the dough into two flat discs. Place one of them between two sheets of cling film and roll out to a thickness of 3 mm. Peel off the top piece of film and use your cutter to stamp out circles or the shape of your choice. Place them on one of the prepared trays, spacing them at least 3 cm apart. Repeat this process with the other piece of dough.

Using a cocktail stick or fine skewer, pierce the biscuits all around the edges. This doesn't just look lovely – it's essential to ensure the biscuits bake evenly. Bake for about 25 minutes, until the biscuits look dry on top and light golden. Leave the biscuits to firm up on their trays for about 10 minutes, then cool on a wire rack.

Once the biscuits are cold, melt the chocolate (see page 6).

Meanwhile, place a sheet of baking paper under the wire rack and turn all your biscuits over. Pour a teaspoonful of melted chocolate onto each of the biscuits and spread with a palette knife to cover the surface evenly. Leave to set for at least an hour.

'Squashed fly' biscuits

There is nothing like a squashed fly (or Garibaldi) biscuit to send me back to being six years old and raiding the biscuit tin when I got home from school. Easy to make and delicious to eat, you will wonder why you haven't been making these biscuits for years.

MAKES ABOUT 24

75 g unsalted butter, softened

75 g icing sugar

1 egg, separated

200 g plain flour, sifted

100 g currants or mixed dried fruit, finely chopped

1 tbsp milk

YOU WILL ALSO NEED

Pizza wheel (optional)

Preheat the oven to 180°C/Mark 4 and line two baking trays with non-stick baking paper.

Cream together the butter and icing sugar. Add the egg white and flour and mix until a dough forms. Gently knead the dough into a ball and divide into two equal pieces.

Lightly flour a work surface and roll out both pieces of dough to a thickness of 5 mm. Put one piece on a large sheet of greaseproof paper and cover it generously with the fruit. Place the other piece of dough on top, squash it down lightly with your hands, then gently use the rolling pin to roll the double layer as thinly as possible. If the fruit starts peeping through, patch it up with your fingers and stop rolling. Trim the edges straight with a pizza wheel or sharp knife and cut into squares approximately 3 x 3 cm.

Beat the egg yolk with the milk and brush this generously over the top of the squares. Place them on the baking trays and bake for 15–20 minutes, until golden and shiny on top. Leave to cool on their trays for about 5 minutes, then use a palette knife to transfer them carefully to a wire rack.

* Miranda's Variations

At Christmas time replace 50 g of the dried fruit with 50 g dried cranberries and add a pinch of cinnamon or mixed spice.

Lemon drizzlers

Heavenly and lemony, these biscuits are rather special. They are finished with a melting drizzle of lemon juice icing that soaks into the biscuit and leaves a pretty glaze – simply divine.

MAKES ABOUT 20

85 g unsalted butter, softened

115 g caster sugar

2 egg yolks

finely grated zest of 1 lemon

175 g plain flour

50 g ground almonds

FOR THE DRIZZLE

80 g icing sugar, sifted

juice of 1 lemon (about 3 tbsp)

Preheat the oven to 180°C/Mark 4 and line two baking trays with non-stick baking paper.

Cream the butter, sugar and lemon zest. Add the egg yolks one at a time and mix well after each addition. Once they are completely combined, add the flour and ground almonds and mix until a dough forms.

With floured hands, roll the dough into walnut-sized balls. Place on the prepared trays, spacing them at least 3 cm apart, and flatten a little with the palm of your hand or the back of a wooden spoon. Bake for 10–15 minutes, or until pale golden.

Meanwhile, make the drizzle by mixing the icing sugar with the lemon juice.

Remove the biscuits from the oven and immediately drizzle a teaspoonful of the lemon icing over each one. Allow the biscuits to cool on their trays for at least 10 minutes, then use a palette knife to transfer them carefully to a wire rack.

✳ Miranda's Variations

For nut-free biscuits, the ground almonds can be replaced with cornflour or plain flour, but the biscuits will not be as moist.

Rainy day gingerbread

Since I was five, I have enjoyed holidays in the Lake District, where I love to buy the wonderful gingerbread made in Sarah Nelson's tiny shop in Grasmere. The smell of her gingerbread cheers even the greyest and wettest day.

MAKES ABOUT 20

125 g plain wholemeal flour

125 g fine oatmeal

125 g demerara sugar

1 tsp ground ginger

½ tsp baking powder

pinch of salt

150 g unsalted butter, at room temperature

40 g mixed peel, finely chopped

40 g crystallised ginger, finely chopped

1 tbsp golden syrup

1 tbsp black treacle

FOR THE TOPPING

1 tbsp plain wholemeal flour

4 tbsp fine oatmeal

1 tsp ground ginger

4 tbsp demerara sugar

Combine the flour, oatmeal, sugar, ground ginger, baking powder and salt in a bowl. Roughly chop the butter and rub into the dry ingredients with your fingers until the mixture resembles fine breadcrumbs. Add the peel and ginger and mix again.

Using a spoon dipped into boiling water, measure the syrup and treacle into a cup. Place in the microwave on High for 10 seconds, then add to the flour mixture and stir until a dough forms.

Tip the dough onto a sheet of cling film and use your hands to shape it into a rectangle about 1 cm thick. Wrap tightly in the cling film and refrigerate for at least 1 hour.

Preheat the oven to 170°C/Mark 3 and line two baking trays with non-stick baking paper.

Place the chilled dough between two sheets of cling film and roll out to a thickness of 5 mm, trying to keep it a rectangular shape. Lift off the cling film and use a sharp knife to cut the dough into rectangles about 7 x 9 cm. Place on the prepared trays, spacing them at least 2 cm apart, and bake for 8 minutes.

Meanwhile, put the topping ingredients into a bowl and mix.

When the biscuits have baked for 8 minutes, remove from the oven and sprinkle them with the topping. Gently press into the surface with the back of a spoon or a large palette knife. Return to the oven and bake for another 5 minutes. The squares should be a darker golden colour than when they went in, but be careful not to overbake them. Leave to cool on their trays for at least 5 minutes, then use a palette knife to transfer them to a wire rack. They will firm up as they cool and should be slightly chewy in the middle.

Orange and sultana Shrewsburys

Homemade Shrewsburys are so much lovelier than their shop-bought relations. Orange zest lends a fresh and light taste, and the sultanas deliver a soft, chewy texture. The biscuits keep brilliantly, and the dough is wonderful to have on standby in the fridge or freezer.

MAKES ABOUT 24

250 g plain flour, sifted

175 g unsalted butter, straight from the fridge

175 g caster sugar

75 g sultanas

zest of 1 orange

1 medium egg yolk

caster sugar, for sprinkling

YOU WILL ALSO NEED

4 cm round metal cutter, preferably fluted

Put the flour into a large mixing bowl. Using the coarse side of a grater, grate the butter into the flour. Rub or process together until the mixture resembles breadcrumbs.

Add the sugar and finely grated orange zest and stir to combine. Mix in the egg yolk and knead or process until a dough forms. It will seem too dry, but resist the temptation to add any more liquid and keep working until it is smooth but still slightly crumbly. Wrap tightly in cling film and flatten into a disc shape with the palm of your hand. Chill for about 1 hour.

Preheat the oven to 190°C/Mark 5 and line two baking trays with non-stick baking paper.

Place the chilled dough between two sheets of cling film and roll out to a thickness of about 3 mm. (Rolling out with flour spoils the delicate texture of the biscuits.) Peel off the top piece of film and use a 4 cm cutter to stamp out circles. Place them on the prepared trays, spacing them at least 3 cm apart, and bake for about 15 minutes, until they are golden brown at the edges and pale golden on top. Sprinkle immediately with caster sugar and press it gently into the surface with the back of a spoon. Leave the biscuits to firm up on the trays for at least 15 minutes, then use a large palette knife to transfer them carefully to a wire rack.

Scrumptious shortbread

This is such a versatile recipe that you can use it to make classic shortbread fingers, or add some of your favourite flavourings. The semolina gives the shortbread an irresistible crispness and helps it to withstand a little dunking.

MAKES ABOUT 24

150 g plain flour

50 g cornflour

2 pinches of salt

100 g semolina

200 g unsalted butter, straight from the fridge

110 g caster sugar

Preheat the oven to 170°C/Mark 3 and line two baking trays with non-stick baking paper.

Sift the flour, cornflour and salt into a large bowl. Add the semolina and grate in the butter, then rub in using your fingertips or process until the mixture resembles large breadcrumbs and starts to form a dough. Stop mixing and bring the dough together with your hands.

Lightly flour a work surface. Squash the dough flat with your fingers, then gently roll out to a thickness of about 5 mm. Cut into 24 fingers about 2 x 8 cm and place on the prepared trays, spacing them at least 3 cm apart. Prick all over with a fork, sprinkle with caster sugar and bake for 20–25 minutes, until the fingers look pale golden on top and slightly darker around the edges.

Remove from the oven and sprinkle with more caster sugar while they are still hot. Leave to cool on their trays for at least 10 minutes, then use a palette knife to transfer them carefully to a wire rack.

* Miranda's Variations

For lemon and white chocolate shortbread rounds, replace the caster sugar with soft light brown sugar and add the finely grated zest of a lemon to the dry ingredients. Roll the dough into a long sausage shape, then wrap in cling film and chill for at least 1 hour. Cut into 1 cm slices and bake for about 20 minutes, or until pale golden. Allow to cool on the trays for about 5 minutes, then transfer to a wire rack. When they are completely cold, melt 200 g of good-quality white chocolate (see page 6) and half-dip the biscuits in it, tidying up the edges with a palette knife. Place on greaseproof or non-stick baking paper to set.

Coconut cherry macaroons

English macaroons may be deemed old-fashioned and less sophisticated than their French namesakes, but they hold a different type of appeal from the alluring designer macarons of Monsieur Hermé. I know some people will shriek at my suggestion that you top them with cherries and dark chocolate, but these additions make a truly delicious combination with the coconut. Give them a chance and you might just get hooked. Oh, and did I mention that they are also far easier to make than most of their French cousins?

MAKES 12

2 egg whites

¼ tsp cream of tartar

140 g caster sugar

200 g shredded or
    desiccated coconut

25 g ground almonds

pinch of salt

6 glacé cherries, halved

50 g dark chocolate, at
    least 70% cocoa solids

YOU WILL ALSO NEED

Rice paper

Small ice-cream scoop
    (optional)

Piping bag

Preheat the oven to 170°C/Mark 3 and line two baking trays with non-stick baking paper. Put sheets of rice paper on top.

Whisk the egg whites and cream of tartar until soft peaks start to form. Add the sugar, about a tablespoon at a time, and whisk until the mixture is glossy. Using a metal spoon or a palette knife, gently fold in the coconut, ground almonds and salt.

Using a small ice-cream scoop or two tablespoons, place neat, heaped dollops of the mixture on the prepared trays, spacing them at least 3–4 cm apart. Gently press half a glacé cherry into the top of each one. Bake for about 20 minutes, or until dry and golden on the outside. Set the macaroons aside on their baking trays and allow to firm up for at least 10 minutes.

Carefully cut around the macaroons, leaving a small circle of rice paper on the bottom of each one. Use a palette knife to transfer them carefully to a wire rack to cool completely.

When ready to decorate, melt the chocolate (see page 6). Allow to cool for about 5 minutes, then spoon into a piping bag and snip off the corner (you need just a tiny hole). Place a sheet of greaseproof or baking paper under the wire rack and drizzle the chocolate over the macaroons. Leave to set.

Custardy creams

I make no apologies for these biscuits not being perfect replicas of the old favourite because this version is heavenly. They are almost better the day after you make them as the filling and biscuit blend together.

MAKES ABOUT 12

60 g icing sugar

170 g unsalted butter, softened

175 g self-raising flour

60 g custard powder

icing sugar, to dust

FOR THE CUSTARD CREAM

1½ tbsp custard powder

1–2 tsp boiling water

50 g unsalted butter, softened

125 g icing sugar, sifted

YOU WILL ALSO NEED

Small ice-cream scoop (optional)

Piping bag (optional)

Preheat the oven to 150°C/Mark 2 and line two baking trays with non-stick baking paper.

Sift the icing sugar into a bowl and mix with the butter until creamy. Sift in the flour and custard powder and mix until a dough forms.

Using a small ice-cream scoop or two tablespoons, place walnut-sized dollops of dough on the prepared trays, spacing them at least 3 cm apart. Flatten gently with the palm of your hand or the back of a wooden spoon and bake for about 15 minutes, or until they look yellow and dry, not golden brown. Keep a close eye on them as they burn really easily. Leave the biscuits to cool on their trays for about 5 minutes, then use a palette knife to transfer them carefully to a wire rack to cool completely.

To make the custard cream, put the custard powder in a bowl and mix to a paste with the boiling water. Add the butter and icing sugar and mix until very creamy. If the mixture seems too dry, add another teaspoon of water. Don't panic if it then appears too wet; just cover with cling film and chill for 1 hour or add a little icing sugar to firm up.

Sandwich the biscuits together with a teaspoonful of the custard cream – the neatest way to do this is with a piping bag with the corner snipped off to give a hole about 1 cm wide. Pipe a circle of filling in the middle of the biscuit, leaving a 1 cm gap around the edge, then gently press another biscuit on top. Dust with icing sugar before serving.

Viennese whirls

These classic biscuits can be made a few days in advance and sandwiched together when you need them. Whisk the filling well to make it light and creamy, and use the best-quality jam.

MAKES ABOUT 10

185 g unsalted butter, softened

50 g icing sugar

seeds from 1 vanilla pod (optional)

175 g plain flour

25 g cornflour

½ tsp baking powder

100 g white chocolate

icing sugar, to dust

FOR THE FILLING

80 g unsalted butter, softened

250 g icing sugar

½ tsp vanilla extract

2 tbsp milk

about 5 tbsp good-quality strawberry jam

YOU WILL ALSO NEED

Piping bag with a large star nozzle (optional)

Preheat the oven to 190°C/Mark 5 and line two baking trays with non-stick baking paper.

Cream the butter, icing sugar and vanilla seeds (if using) until light and fluffy, ideally for about 2 minutes on a high speed in the mixer. Scrape down the sides of the bowl, then sift in the flour, cornflour and baking powder and beat again until very creamy.

Spoon the mixture into a piping bag fitted with a large star nozzle and pipe spirals of dough, about 3 cm across and 3 cm apart, onto the prepared trays. Bake for about 10 minutes, or until firm to the touch and pale golden. Cool on their trays for 10 minutes, then use a palette knife to transfer them carefully to a wire rack.

Once the biscuits are completely cold, place a sheet of baking paper under the rack. Melt the chocolate (see page 6), then brush a thin layer of it over the bottom of each biscuit – this will prevent them from going soggy when they have been filled.

To make the filling, beat together the butter, icing sugar and vanilla. Add the milk a little at a time, whisking for 2–3 minutes to make it creamy and fluffy.

Once the chocolate is completely set, put the buttercream into a piping bag fitted with a large star nozzle and pipe a spiral of it onto the chocolate side of half the biscuits, keeping it about 1 cm away from the edge. Alternatively, use a teaspoon to add the buttercream if you prefer. Spread jam on the chocolate side of the remaining biscuits, then sandwich the jammy and creamy halves together. Chill for about 30 minutes to firm up the filling.

Dust generously with icing sugar and serve in individual cupcake cases or on a pretty cake-stand.

Fudgy nut conversation stoppers

Here is a biscuit that will make even the most dedicated chatterer pause for breath. They are very more-ish and, once bitten into, just have to be finished. They taste as homely and delicious as they look, and the combination of fudge and hazelnut makes them biscuits full of comfort. Let your companions think you have slaved for hours over these creations, safe in the knowledge that you have dough ready in the freezer to make another batch whenever a chatterbox calls.

MAKES AT LEAST 16

200 g plain flour

1 tsp salt

½ tsp bicarbonate of soda

125 g unsalted butter, at room temperature

125 g light muscovado sugar

1 egg, lightly beaten

1 tsp vanilla extract

175 g toasted hazelnuts (see page 7), 125 g roughly chopped and 50 g finely chopped

100 g good-quality vanilla fudge

icing sugar, to dust

Sift the flour, salt and bicarbonate of soda into a bowl. Rub in the butter with your fingers or whizz in a food processor until the mixture looks like coarse breadcrumbs. Add the sugar, egg, vanilla, 75 g of the coarsely chopped nuts plus the 50 g of finely chopped nuts and half the fudge and mix together until a dough forms. Roll into a log shape on a lightly floured work surface, then wrap tightly in cling film and chill for at least 1 hour. (The dough could be frozen at this point for future use.)

Preheat the oven to 190°C/Mark 5 and line two baking trays with non-stick baking paper.

Cut the chilled dough into slices about 1 cm thick. Place them on the prepared trays, spacing them at least 3 cm apart. Sprinkle a generous amount of the remaining nuts and fudge onto each biscuit and press into the dough with your fingers. Bake for about 12 minutes, or until golden around the edges.

Leave the biscuits to cool on their baking trays for at least 10 minutes, then use a palette knife to transfer them carefully to a wire rack. When cold, dust with icing sugar and serve.

Chocolate flapjack biscuits

Inspired by my mother's flapjacks, which she always topped with chocolate, I've devised this delicious oaty, syrupy biscuit that is also smothered in chocolate. What could be more perfect to enjoy with a cup of tea? Plain flapjack will look naked from now on!

MAKES AT LEAST 16

125 g self-raising flour

pinch of salt

½ tsp bicarbonate of soda

75 g porridge oats

75 g demerara sugar

50 g very finely chopped
apricots (optional)

100 g unsalted butter

1 tbsp golden syrup

100 g milk chocolate, at
least 54% cocoa solids

Preheat the oven to 180°C/Mark 4 and line two baking trays with non-stick baking paper.

Sift the flour, salt and bicarbonate of soda into a large bowl. Add the oats, sugar and apricots (if using) and mix together with a wooden spoon.

Put the butter and golden syrup into a large pan and melt over a low heat, stirring all the time. Remove from the heat and tip the oat mixture into the pan. Stir until well combined.

With floured hands, make walnut-sized balls of dough and place them on the prepared trays, spacing them at least 3 cm apart. Carefully flatten each biscuit with the blade of a large palette knife or the palm of your hand. Bake for 20 minutes or until golden brown. Leave to cool on their trays for about 10 minutes, then use a palette knife to transfer them carefully to a wire rack.

When the biscuits are completely cold, melt the chocolate (see page 6). Put a sheet of greaseproof or baking paper under the wire rack, then use a palette knife to smooth a thin layer of chocolate over the top of each biscuit. Leave to set at room temperature, or pop them into the fridge if you need to eat them urgently.

3 SEASONAL BISCUITS

Biscuits can be in tune with the seasons. Taste and smell are tied up with our experiences of what happens at certain times of the year. The whiff of bonfire smoke or the first buds of spring, for example, can conjure up potent memories and remind us of things traditionally eaten at those times.

Some biscuits remind me of holidays or places I have been. Others relate to special celebrations or ancient traditions. Many of them exploit seasonal produce and will, I hope, encourage you to experiment with ingredients and biscuit recipes in a different way.

I hope that some of these recipes will become personal or family favourites, and that enjoying these biscuits together will create memories that last a lifetime.

Spring
Lemon and almond knots

Crunchy twists of lemony almond dough sprinkled with sugar and flaked almonds or drizzled with lemon icing — these fresh and zesty biscuits are perfect for celebrating the arrival of spring.

MAKES ABOUT 12

125 g unsalted butter, softened

40 g soft light brown sugar

25 g caster sugar

1 egg, lightly beaten

1 tsp lemon juice

½ tsp almond extract

180 g plain flour, sifted

40 g ground almonds

25 g flaked almonds, toasted (see page 7)

FOR THE ICING

100 g icing sugar, sifted

zest of ½ a lemon

3 tsp lemon juice

YOU WILL ALSO NEED

Pastry brush

Piping bag (optional)

Cream together the butter and sugars. Add all but 2 teaspoons of the egg, plus the lemon juice and almond extract and beat well to combine. Add the flour, ground almonds and lemon zest and mix until a dough forms. Shape into a fat log about 4 cm in diameter, wrap tightly in cling film and chill for at least 1 hour.

Line two baking trays with non-stick baking paper.

Dust your hands and the work surface with flour. Cut a thick 3 cm slice off the chilled dough, roll it into a long, thin sausage shape, then wind into a figure-of-eight knot shape. Carefully lift onto a prepared tray. Repeat until all the dough has been used up, or freeze half of it to make more knots on another day. Put the filled trays in the fridge for about 30 minutes.

Preheat the oven to 200°C/Mark 6.

Brush half the knots with the remaining beaten egg. Crush the toasted almonds in your hands and sprinkle them over the egg glaze. Leave the rest of the knots unglazed. Bake for 12–15 minutes, until they look golden and the surface feels dry. Leave them on their trays to firm up for at least 10 minutes, then use a palette knife to transfer them carefully to a wire rack.

Mix together the icing sugar, lemon zest and juice to make a runny icing. When the biscuits are completely cold, put a sheet of greaseproof paper under the wire rack. Fill a piping bag or freezer bag with the icing, snip a tiny bit off the corner and pipe zigzags across the biscuits. Alternatively, drizzle the icing over with a spoon. Leave to harden.

Passionate chocolate hearts

What better way to convey your love or romantic feelings than with these melt-in-the-mouth shortbread hearts sandwiched with white chocolate and passion-fruit ganache?

MAKES ABOUT 12

170 g unsalted butter, softened

85 g golden caster sugar

seeds from 1 vanilla pod

50 g white chocolate, grated

175 g plain flour, sifted

80 g rice flour, sifted

pinch of salt

15 g caster sugar

15 g freeze-dried raspberries or toasted flaked almonds (optional)

icing sugar, to dust

FOR THE FILLING

100 ml double cream

200 g white chocolate, finely chopped

1 tbsp unsalted butter, softened

pulp from 4 passion-fruit

YOU WILL ALSO NEED

Heart-shaped cutter

Cream the butter, sugar and vanilla seeds, then mix in the chocolate. (If using a food processor, you can chop the chocolate in it first, then add the butter, sugar and vanilla, and cream them all together.) Add both the flours and the salt, then mix until a dough forms. Bring it together with your hands and knead gently. Squash the dough into two flat discs, wrap tightly in cling film and chill for about 30 minutes.

Preheat the oven to 180°C/Mark 4 and line two baking trays with non-stick baking paper.

Squash the chilled dough a little to soften it, then place each disc between two sheets of cling film and roll out to a thickness of 3 mm. Use your cutter to stamp out 24 heart shapes. Place them on the prepared trays, spacing them at least 3 cm apart, and chill for about 10 minutes. Bake for 10–15 minutes, less if the hearts are very small, until lightly golden and quite firm.

While still hot on their trays, sprinkle half the biscuits with caster sugar and some of the crumbled raspberries or flaked almonds (if using). Leave the biscuits to cool completely.

To make the filling, heat the cream until it is just boiling, then pour over the chocolate and beat vigorously with a wooden spoon. Allow to cool and thicken a little before beating in the butter. Fold in the passion-fruit a little at a time as you do not want to make the ganache too runny – you might not need all the pulp.

Spread a dollop of ganache on the underside of a plain biscuit, then gently press a raspberry- or almond-covered biscuit on top. Repeat until all the biscuits are sandwiched together. Dust with icing sugar and enjoy.

Rhubarb crumble biscuits

I like to make these biscuits as soon as we spot the first shoots of rhubarb in the garden. The rhubarb is chopped straight into the biscuit dough, and orange zest is added to intensify its flavour. If you are a fan of rhubarb crumble, these biscuits will certainly hit the spot.

MAKES AT LEAST 12

115 g unsalted butter, softened

115 g demerara sugar

1 large egg

180 g plain flour

1 tsp vanilla extract

zest of ½ an orange

½ tsp bicarbonate of soda

150 g fresh rhubarb, chopped into 1 cm pieces

FOR THE CRUMBLE

30 g unsalted butter, softened

30 g plain flour

40 g demerara sugar

20 g caster sugar

1 tsp orange zest

YOU WILL ALSO NEED

Small ice-cream scoop (optional)

Preheat the oven to 180°C/Mark 4 and line two baking trays with non-stick baking paper.

Cream together the butter and sugar, then beat in the egg. Add the flour, vanilla and orange zest and mix gently until combined. Fold the rhubarb into the mixture.

Using a small ice-cream scoop or two tablespoons, put 12 dollops of the mixture onto the prepared trays, spacing them at least 3 cm apart. Bake for 10 minutes.

Meanwhile, make the crumble topping: rub the butter into the flour using your fingers, then stir in the other ingredients.

Take the biscuits out of the oven, flatten them a little with a palette knife, then put about 1 tablespoon of crumble on top of each one. Return to the oven and bake for a further 5 minutes, or until golden around the edges. Leave on the trays to cool. These biscuits are best eaten the day you make them.

M-M-M-Maltesers® biscuits

These comforting biscuits are great to make when your cupboards are almost bare because the recipe requires only a few ingredients and no eggs. They are perfect biscuits for springtime, when you are trying to be good but need a light chocolate fix.

MAKES ABOUT 16

85 g unsalted butter, softened

100 g granulated sugar

60 ml milk

50 g Horlicks Original

125 g plain flour

½ tsp bicarbonate of soda

¼ tsp baking powder

¼ tsp salt

80 g Maltesers®, chopped in half

YOU WILL ALSO NEED

Small ice-cream scoop (optional)

Preheat the oven to 180°C/Mark 4 and line two baking trays with non-stick baking paper.

Cream together the butter and sugar, then add the milk and beat well to combine. Add the flour (on a low speed if using a mixer), the bicarbonate of soda, baking powder and salt. Finally, fold in the Maltesers.

Using a small ice-cream scoop or two tablespoons, put 16 dollops of the dough onto the prepared baking trays, spacing them at least 3 cm apart. Bake for 10 minutes, then check their progress: if they are not golden, return them to the oven for a few more minutes.

Leave to firm up on the baking trays for at least 10 minutes, then use a palette knife to transfer them carefully to a wire rack. Eat while still warm or allow to cool completely.

Easter nests

It is not only children who will love making and eating these little chocolate nests filled with tiny eggs. They look very pretty on a cake-stand decorated with fluffy yellow chicks.

MAKES 12

75 g milk chocolate

75 g dark chocolate

2 Mars bars

50 g unsalted butter

2 tsp golden syrup

about 5 Shredded Wheat, crumbled

36 mini chocolate eggs

YOU WILL ALSO NEED

Fluffy yellow chicks, to decorate

Line a baking tray with non-stick baking paper, or put paper cases into a 12-hole cupcake tray. Set aside.

Break the chocolate into pieces and chop the Mars bars into small slices. Put them all into a pan with the butter and syrup and melt over a low heat, stirring regularly to make sure the mixture doesn't stick or burn. Set aside to cool for a few minutes.

Stir about a third of the Shredded Wheat into the melted chocolate and mix really well. Continue adding the Shredded Wheat a little at a time and mixing after each addition. Stop adding if it looks like there is not enough chocolate to cover any more.

Spoon 12 dollops of the mixture onto the baking tray or into the paper cases. Make a dent in the middle with your fingertip or the handle of a wooden spoon and press three eggs into it while still wet. Put the tray in the fridge for a few hours or ideally overnight. Sit a fluffy chick on top of some of the nests before serving.

Hot-cross biscuits

Inspired by hot-cross buns, these biscuits are full of spices, citrussy flavours and fruit.

MAKES ABOUT 18

125 g unsalted butter, softened

50 g caster sugar

25 g soft light brown sugar

2 tsp finely grated orange zest

2 tsp finely grated lemon zest

1 egg yolk

100 g plain white flour

50 g plain wholemeal flour

25 g cornflour

½ tsp ground cinnamon

½ tsp ground ginger

¼ tsp ground mixed spice

40 g currants

40 g sultanas

20 g mixed peel

3 tsp apricot jam

50 g icing sugar

1 tsp freshly squeezed orange juice

YOU WILL ALSO NEED

7 cm round metal cutter

Disposable piping bag (optional)

Preheat the oven to 200°C/Mark 6 and line two baking trays with non-stick baking paper.

Cream the butter, sugars and zests. Add the egg yolk and beat well.

Sift together the flours, cornflour and spices and add to the butter and egg mixture along with the dried fruit and peel and the bran left in the sieve. Mix well to combine and form a dough. Put the dough between two sheets of cling film and gently roll out to a thickness of about 5 mm.

Use a 7 cm cutter to stamp out 18 circles. Place them on the prepared trays, spacing them at least 2 cm apart, then bake for 10 minutes. Meanwhile, gently warm the apricot jam and 1 tablespoon water in a small pan. After 10 minutes, brush the top of the biscuits with the apricot glaze. Return them to the oven to bake for a further 5 minutes, or until golden. Allow to cool on their trays for 10 minutes, then use a palette knife to transfer them carefully to a wire rack.

Once the biscuits are completely cold, mix together the icing sugar and orange juice. Spoon into a piping bag or freezer bag, snip off the corner to give a hole about 2 mm wide, and pipe a cross on top of each biscuit. Leave to set.

* Miranda's Variations

To make Simnel biscuits, omit the icing and roll out a piece of marzipan to a thickness of 2–3 mm. Stamp out 18 circles with the same cutter used for the biscuits. When the biscuits have been brushed with the apricot glaze, press a marzipan circle on top, return to the oven and bake for about 5 more minutes.

Chocolate brownie biscuits

Dense, fudgy like a brownie and incredibly chocolatey, these biscuits can almost be turned into a pudding by pressing a raspberry into the heart of each one before baking. Two types of dark chocolate are needed to give them their intense flavour.

MAKES ABOUT 24

100 g Bournville chocolate

150 g dark chocolate, at least 70% cocoa solids

75 g unsalted butter

180 g caster sugar

3 large eggs, whisked

1 tsp vanilla extract

125 g plain flour, sifted

¼ tsp sea salt

75 g white chocolate, at least 25% cocoa solids, cut into chunks

50 g milk chocolate, cut into chunks

150 g raspberries (optional)

cocoa powder, to dust

Put the Bournville and 100g of the 70% dark chocolate into a bowl with the butter and melt over a pan of simmering water. Set aside to cool for about 10 minutes.

Preheat the oven to 190°C/Mark 5 and line two baking trays with non-stick baking paper.

Using a mixer on high speed, beat the chocolate mixture with the sugar for about 2 minutes. Add the eggs and beat on a high speed for about another 3 minutes. It is really important to get lots of air into the mixture, as this will give the biscuits their gorgeous brownie crust. Beat in the vanilla, then gently fold in the flour and salt using a large metal spoon. Finally, fold in all but a handful of the white and milk chocolate chunks. Let the mixture stand for 5–10 minutes in a cool place (not the fridge) to firm up a bit.

Using two tablespoons, place 24 generous dollops of the chocolate mixture on the prepared trays, spacing them at least 3 cm apart. Place a few of the remaining milk and white chocolate chunks on top of each biscuit and press a raspberry (if using) into the middle.

Bake for about 10 minutes, until the surface looks dry and flaky, like brownies. Leave to firm up for a few minutes, then use a palette knife to transfer them carefully to a plate and devour immediately. Alternatively, if you aren't eating the biscuits straight away and want to keep the middle of them wonderfully squidgy, put the baking tray straight into the fridge to stop them cooking and leave for about 30 minutes. I like to dust them with cocoa powder before serving.

Summer
Berry cheesecake thumbprints

Tiny cups of buttery biscuit encircling miniature strawberry and redcurrant cheesecakes ... what better way to celebrate summer?

MAKES 24

200 g unsalted butter, softened

100 g caster sugar

1 egg yolk

300 g plain flour, sifted

¼ tsp salt

FOR THE FILLING

110 g cream cheese

100 g caster sugar

1 egg yolk

2 tsp double cream

seeds from 1 vanilla pod

pinch of salt

100 g redcurrants

100 g strawberries, finely chopped

TO DECORATE

icing sugar

sprigs of redcurrants

mint leaves

Preheat the oven to 180°C/Mark 4 and line two baking trays with non-stick baking paper.

First make the filling. Put all the ingredients, except the fruit, into a bowl and beat together. Cover with cling film and chill for at least 30 minutes.

To make the biscuits, cream the butter and sugar, then beat in the egg yolk. Add the flour and salt and mix until a dough forms.

Using two tablespoons, put 24 dollops of the dough onto the prepared trays, spacing them at least 3 cm apart. Alternatively, use your hands to roll the dough into walnut-sized balls and arrange these on the trays. Dip your thumb in flour and make a dent in the centre of each dollop or ball. Try to make the dents as large as possible while keeping a reasonable wall of dough around the edge. The dollops should look like thumb-pots made from clay.

Bake for 8 minutes, then use the handle of a wooden spoon to reopen the holes. Return the trays to the oven and bake for another 8–10 minutes, or until pale golden. Leave the biscuits to cool for about 10 minutes on their trays.

Put about 6 redcurrants and some chopped strawberries into the hole in each biscuit, then spoon in the filling. Put two or three redcurrants on top, then bake for a further 7–10 minutes, or until the filling is firm and lightly golden.

Leave the biscuits to cool, then chill for about 4 hours. Just before serving, dust with icing sugar and decorate with sprigs of redcurrants and a few mint leaves.

Lovely lavender biscuits

Delicately scented with lavender flowers, these pretty biscuits remind me of walking through a beautiful garden on a perfect summer's day. You can almost feel yourself relaxing as you eat them.

MAKES ABOUT 18

1 heaped tbsp lavender
    flowers (no stalks)
175 g self-raising flour,
    sifted
50 g caster sugar
pinch of salt
25 g semolina
130 g unsalted butter,
    straight from the
    fridge
caster sugar, for
    sprinkling

YOU WILL ALSO NEED

5 cm heart-shaped or
    round cutter

Put the lavender and flour into a food processor and chop finely. Add the sugar, salt and semolina and whizz to combine. Finely chop or coarsely grate the butter into the mixture and whizz again until a dough forms. Squash into a flat disc, wrap tightly in cling film and chill for at least 30 minutes.

Preheat the oven to 180°C/Mark 4 and line two baking trays with non-stick baking paper.

Place the chilled dough between two sheets of fresh cling film and roll out to a thickness of 3–4 mm. Using a 5 cm cutter, stamp out hearts or circles. Place on the prepared trays, spacing them at least 3 cm apart, and sprinkle with caster sugar. Bake for 15–20 minutes, or less if the biscuits are very small. Sprinkle generously with caster sugar straight after taking them out of the oven, and leave to cool.

Tip: To make round biscuits without using a cutter, roll the dough into a log 5–6 cm in diameter, then wrap and chill as before. Cut into slices about 4 mm thick and bake as above, sprinkling with caster sugar before and after baking.

Hazelnut thins

Simple, buttery biscuits packed with toasted hazelnuts, these thins are lovely with rhubarb fool and add a homemade twist to bowls of fruit and ice cream.

MAKES ABOUT 20

110 g unsalted butter, softened

55 g soft light brown sugar

170 g plain flour, sifted

120 g hazelnuts, toasted and ground (see page 7)

YOU WILL ALSO NEED

4–5 cm round cutter

Preheat the oven to 160°C/Mark 3 and line two baking trays with non-stick baking paper.

Cream together the butter and sugar. Add the flour and all but 1 tablespoon of the hazelnuts. Mix well until a dough forms. Wrap tightly in cling film and chill for 30 minutes.

Place the chilled dough between two fresh sheets of cling film and roll out as thinly as you can. Using a 4–5 cm round cutter, stamp out circles, then use a palette knife to lift them carefully onto the prepared trays, spacing them at least 3 cm apart. Sprinkle with the remaining hazelnuts and press gently into the surface of the dough. Bake for 15–20 minutes, until light golden brown and slightly darker around the edges. Set the biscuits aside to cool on their trays for 10 minutes, then use a palette knife to transfer them carefully to a wire rack to cool completely.

✳ Miranda's Variations

Sandwich the biscuits together with a hazelnut chocolate ganache. To make this, put 150 ml double cream into a bowl set over a pan of simmering water. Break 150 g dark chocolate (ideally Bournville) into small pieces and add to the cream, stirring until melted and combined. Remove from the heat and stir in 100 g toasted and roughly chopped hazelnuts. Leave to cool until thick and spreadable, then use to sandwich the biscuits together.

Strawberry ricotta biscuits

Fresh strawberries are wonderful in these delicate, almost cake-like biscuits, but other soft fruits can be used if you prefer. Everyone who has tasted these has begged me for the recipe.

MAKES AT LEAST 18

110 g unsalted butter, softened

200 g caster sugar

1 tsp vanilla extract

seeds from 1 vanilla pod

1 egg

225 g ricotta cheese

250 g plain flour, preferably superfine or '00'

½ tsp bicarbonate of soda

¼ tsp salt

125 g strawberries, wiped clean (not washed) and chopped

9 strawberries, cut in half, to decorate

FOR THE ICING

100 g icing sugar

2 strawberries, pushed through a sieve

Preheat the oven to 180°C/Mark 4 and line two baking trays with non-stick baking paper.

Cream the butter and sugar with the vanilla extract and seeds until light and fluffy – about 2 minutes in a mixer. Beat in the egg, then fold in the ricotta using a metal spoon and mix gently to combine. Sift the dry ingredients and fold into the mixture. Finally, fold in the chopped strawberries.

Use two tablespoons to place dollops of the mixture on the prepared trays, spacing them at least 3–4 cm apart. Bake for 10–15 minutes, or until the edges are golden. Leave the biscuits to cool on their trays for about 10 minutes, then use a palette knife to transfer them carefully to a wire rack.

When the biscuits are completely cold, mix the icing ingredients in a bowl. You can add a little water if the icing's consistency is too stiff.; it should be smooth but not too runny.

Slide a sheet of greaseproof paper under the rack, then use a spoon to drizzle the icing over the biscuits. You can either decorate with the halved strawberries and serve straight away, or leave the icing to set and serve the biscuits with fresh strawberries on the side.

✱ Miranda's Variations

Replace the strawberries with 2 tsp lemon zest and press a whole raspberry into the middle of each biscuit before baking.

Roulade biscuits

This recipe is a wonderful combination of summery flavours — raspberries and meringue — all rolled up in a biscuit.

MAKES AT LEAST 24

120 g unsalted butter, straight from the fridge, chopped into small pieces

150 g plain flour

20 g ground almonds

50 g caster sugar

pinch of salt

1 egg yolk

FOR THE FILLING

100 g fresh raspberries, slightly squashed

2 large egg whites

½ tsp cream of tartar

100 g caster sugar

Rub the butter into the flour until the mixture resembles coarse breadcrumbs, then add the almonds, sugar, salt and butter. Add the egg yolk and mix to make a sticky dough. Shape into a disc, then wrap tightly in cling film and chill for at least 1 hour.

Meanwhile, make the meringue. Whisk the egg whites with the cream of tartar until stiff. Add the sugar in about four goes, whisking well after each addition, until the mixture is very glossy.

Preheat the oven to 190°C/Mark 5 and line a large baking tray with non-stick baking paper.

Place the chilled dough between two sheets of greaseproof paper and roll into a rectangle about 1 cm thick. Transfer the dough, still on its paper, to the lined tray and carefully peel off the top sheet of greaseproof. Bake in the oven for about 5 minutes, then cool for about 10 minutes before squashing the raspberries over the top of the dough. Spread a layer of meringue over the fruit, then return to the oven and bake for 15 minutes, until golden. Remove from the oven and lower the temperature to 150°C/Mark 2.

Allow the dough to cool for about 2 minutes, then roll it up like a Swiss roll, using the paper to help you, then pulling it away as you roll. The dough will be quite sticky, so this process will seem a bit messy, but don't worry if it looks scruffy or a bit broken at this stage.

Put the dough back in the oven and bake for another 20 minutes. Remove again, and reduce the temperature to 110°C/Mark ¼. Sprinkle the roll with caster sugar and leave to cool on the tray for about 5 minutes before cutting into 3 mm slices with a sharp knife. Carefully lay the slices on the tray and return to the oven for a further 30 minutes. Cool on the trays for at least 10 minutes, then transfer the biscuits to a wire rack until completely cold.

Redcurrant and lemon clouds

Here the lightest, meltingly good lemon biscuits are topped with a pretty puff of redcurrant meringue. The sharpness of the redcurrant is a lovely burst of freshness next to the sweet, buttery biscuit.

MAKES ABOUT 16

100 g unsalted butter, softened

50 g icing sugar

50 g caster sugar

zest of ½ a lemon

1 egg yolk

150 g self-raising flour

50 g cornflour

2 tsp lemon juice

FOR THE TOPPING

2 egg whites

125 g caster sugar

2 tsp cornflour

200 g redcurrants

YOU WILL ALSO NEED

5–6 cm round cutter

Cream together the butter, sugars and lemon zest until light and fluffy. Beat in the egg yolk. Sift in the flour and cornflour, add the lemon juice and mix until a dough starts to form. Using your hands, shape the dough into two large flat discs. Wrap tightly in cling film and chill for at least 30 minutes.

Preheat the oven to 180°C/Mark 4 and line two baking trays with non-stick baking paper.

Place each piece of chilled dough between two fresh sheets of cling film and roll out to a thickness of 3–5 mm. Using a 5–6 cm cutter, stamp out circles of dough. Place on the prepared trays, spacing them at least 3 cm apart, and bake for 10 minutes, or until pale golden.

Meanwhile, prepare the topping. Whisk the egg whites into stiff peaks. Add the sugar and cornflour and whisk on a fast speed for about 4 more minutes. Gently fold in the redcurrants, taking care not to squash too many.

Remove the biscuits from the oven, put a generous spoonful of topping on each one and spread it out a little to cover most of the biscuit base. Return to the oven and bake for a further 10–12 minutes. Leave the biscuits to cool on their trays and eat them the day they are made.

Elderflower moments

For me, the start of summer is when the white confetti of elderflower blossom is heavy on the trees and its sweet, heady smell fills the air. These biscuits capture that first sunny breath of the hot days ahead. Simple, pretty and dusted in white icing sugar, they can make wonderful petit fours or a delicate summery addition to a tea party.

MAKES AT LEAST 24

300 g unsalted butter, softened

55 g icing sugar

4 tsp elderflower cordial

250 g plain flour

50 g cornflour

YOU WILL ALSO NEED

Small ice-cream scoop (optional)

Cream together the butter and icing sugar until very smooth – about 2 minutes in a mixer. Stop after 1 minute and scrape down the sides of the bowl before beating again. Add half the elderflower cordial and beat again.

Sift in the flour and cornflour and mix gently until incorporated. Cover the bowl with cling film and chill for 2 hours.

Preheat the oven to 170°C/Mark 3 and line two baking trays with baking paper.

Using a small ice-cream scoop or two tablespoons, place walnut-sized balls of the chilled dough on the prepared trays, spacing them at least 3 cm apart. Bake for 15 minutes, then remove from the oven and drizzle a little of the remaining elderflower cordial over each biscuit. Return to the oven to bake for a further 3–5 minutes, until golden around the edges.

Allow the biscuits to cool on their trays for 10 minutes, then use a palette knife to transfer them carefully to a wire rack. When completely cold, slide a sheet of greaseproof paper under the rack and dredge the biscuits with icing sugar using a sieve or shaker.

* Miranda's Variations

To make these biscuits even more indulgent, you can sandwich them together with delicious elderflower buttercream. Put 100 g unsalted butter into a bowl with 2 tsp elderflower cordial, 1 tsp lemon zest, 20 ml semi-skimmed milk and 125 g sifted icing sugar. Beat by hand or machine for about 2 minutes, until really creamy. Sift in another 125 g icing sugar and beat for another minute. Keep somewhere cool until needed – not in the fridge, as the mixture will go solid.

Lemonade quenchers

There is something so nostalgic about the taste of homemade lemonade. My mother used to make huge jugs for us to glug in the garden on scorching hot days. Sharp, yet sugary, it really is the most perfect taste of summertime. In these biscuits I have used the whole lemon – skin, pith and flesh – to recreate the same zingy, almost bitter, taste.

MAKES ABOUT 24

1 large lemon

225 g unsalted butter, softened

200 g caster sugar

1 large egg yolk

250 g plain flour

1 tsp bicarbonate of soda

1 tsp cream of tartar

½ tsp salt

FOR ROLLING

zest of 1 lemon

200 g granulated sugar

YOU WILL ALSO NEED

Small ice-cream scoop (optional)

Roughly chop the lemon, discard the pips, then whizz to a pulp in a food processor or blender.

Cream together the butter and sugar until light and fluffy. Add the egg yolk and lemon pulp and beat again, scraping down the sides of the bowl to ensure everything is combined.

Sift in the dry ingredients and stir well. Cover the bowl with cling film and leave to chill for at least 2 hours, but preferably overnight.

Preheat the oven to 180°C/Mark 4 and line two baking trays with non-stick baking paper.

Combine the lemon zest and sugar in a bowl. Using a small ice-cream scoop or two tablespoons, drop balls of the chilled dough into the bowl, rolling them around to ensure they are completely covered. Place on the prepared trays, spacing them at least 3 cm apart, and bake for 12–15 minutes. Leave the biscuits to cool and harden on their trays.

Breton biscuits

Just one bite of these gloriously simple, yet utterly delicious biscuits takes me back to the hot Brittany beaches, where as children we devoured them with dripping fresh peaches from the morning market after swimming in the sea.

MAKES ABOUT 24

200 g unsalted butter, softened

120 g caster sugar

3 egg yolks

370 g superfine flour

pinch of fine sea salt

1 egg yolk mixed with 1 tsp water, to glaze

YOU WILL ALSO NEED

5 cm fluted pastry cutter

Pastry brush

Cream together the butter, sugar and egg yolks, ideally in a mixer at high speed, for 2–3 minutes. Stop about halfway through to scrape down the sides of the bowl. The mixture should be light, creamy and voluminous.

Sift the flour and salt into the mixture and beat again on a lower speed, until a soft dough forms. Using your hands, shape the dough into two large flat discs, wrap tightly in cling film and chill for about 30 minutes.

Preheat the oven to 160°C/Mark 3 and line two baking trays with non-stick baking paper.

Lightly sprinkle a work surface with the same type of flour used to make the biscuits and roll out the dough to a thickness of 3–5 mm. Stamp out circles using a 5 cm fluted cutter. Use a small, sharp knife to lightly slash the back of each circle before laying it cut-side down on the prepared trays. Space the circles about 3 cm apart.

Brush the glaze over the biscuits, then set aside to rest for 5 minutes. Glaze again, then use a knife to cut a deep cross-hatched pattern into the top of the biscuits. Bake for about 15 minutes, or until lightly golden. Set aside to cool on their trays for about 10 minutes, then use a palette knife to transfer them carefully to a wire rack. Leave until completely cold.

Lady's kisses

Known as *baci di dama* in their country of origin, these delicate Italian biscuits are so elegant that friends will think you have brought them back from a pasticceria in Piedmont, where they are said to have first been created. They are easy to make and wonderful with a simple bowl of strawberries or ice cream.

MAKES ABOUT 20

75 g ground almonds

50 g whole almonds, toasted (see page 7)

125 g caster sugar

125 g unsalted butter, softened and roughly chopped

1 tsp vanilla extract

pinch of salt

125 g plain flour, sifted

200 g dark chocolate, at least 70% cocoa solids, broken into small pieces

Preheat the oven to 180°C/Mark 4 and line two baking trays with non-stick baking paper.

Put the ground and whole almonds in a food processor with 2 teaspoons of the caster sugar and whizz to make a fine powder. If you don't have a food processor, replace 25 g of the caster sugar with icing sugar and replace the whole almonds with more ground almonds.

Add the butter, vanilla, salt and remaining caster sugar to the mixture and cream together. Whizz or stir in the flour until well combined and a dough starts to form.

Using your hands, roll the dough into 20 cherry-sized balls and place on the prepared trays, spacing them at least 3 cm apart. Bake for 10–15 minutes, or until golden brown. Leave to cool on the trays for about 5 minutes, then use a palette knife to transfer them to a wire rack.

When the biscuits are completely cold, melt the chocolate (see page 6). Allow to cool a little, then spread about a teaspoonful over the underside of one biscuit and pop another biscuit on top to make a sandwich. Place on a sheet of greaseproof paper and repeat with the remaining biscuits. Try to resist eating them until the chocolate has completely set.

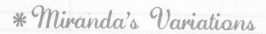

✳ Miranda's Variations

Use toasted ground hazelnuts instead of almonds, or a mixture of hazelnuts and almonds.

Blackcurrant and white chocolate biscuits

In this recipe tart blackcurrants are complemented perfectly by creamy white chocolate and a meltingly good biscuit base. These biscuits look stunning – the pale golden crust is puddled with oozing blackcurrants that gently bleed into the dough and burst with flavour when you bite into them. This is a great way to use a wonderful but often overlooked summer fruit.

MAKES ABOUT 16

225 g unsalted butter, softened

225 g caster sugar

170 g condensed milk

350 g self-raising flour, sifted

150 g white chocolate, at least 25% cocoa solids, chopped into chunks

175 g blackcurrants, topped and tailed

YOU WILL ALSO NEED

Small ice-cream scoop (optional)

Preheat the oven to 180°C/Mark 4 and line two baking trays with non-stick baking paper.

Cream the butter and sugar until light and fluffy. Stir in the condensed milk, then add the flour and mix until a soft dough forms. Mix in the chocolate chunks until evenly distributed. Just before you are ready to use the dough, very gently stir in the blackcurrants, trying not to squash too many. If you do this too far in advance, the blackcurrants will bleed too much into the mixture.

Using a small ice-cream scoop or two tablespoons, put about 16 dollops of dough onto the prepared trays, spacing them at least 3 cm apart. Flatten them slightly with your hand and bake for 15–20 minutes, or until golden brown around the edges. Set aside to firm up on their trays for at least 10 minutes, then use a palette knife to transfer them to a wire rack and leave until completely cold.

Ice cream sandwiches

Everyone likes ice cream, but it's a step closer to heaven when sandwiched between two delicious biscuits. In Scotland these sandwiches are called 'sliders', in New York the chocolate chip version is known as a 'chipwich', and in Australia the usual name is a 'cream between' or 'Eskimo pie'. Indulgent, chilly and good fun, these sandwiches must be eaten the day you make them.

MAKES 8

16 homemade biscuits of your choice (the vanilla and chocolate biscuits on pages 182–183 work well)

8 scoops good-quality ice cream, sorbet or frozen yoghurt

toppings, such as sprinkles, grated chocolate, chopped nuts or crumbled honeycomb

100 g good-quality chocolate (optional)

icing sugar, to dust (optional)

YOU WILL ALSO NEED
Standard ice-cream scoop (optional)

If your biscuit tin is empty and you're making the dough from scratch, roll it out a little thinner than usual (2–3 mm) before cutting into shapes. Keep an eye on the biscuits while they are baking as they will need a little less time than specified. Allow to cool before using them.

Take the ice cream out of the freezer and leave to soften at room temperature for about 5 minutes. Alternatively, defrost in the microwave, but check every 10 seconds because it should be soft and spreadable, not melted.

Line a baking tray with non-stick baking paper and place in the freezer (or, if you are pushed for space, put the paper directly on the shelf, cutting it to the size you have available). Put your toppings into shallow bowls.

Using an ice-cream scoop, put a dollop of softened ice cream on the underside of one of the biscuits, or spread it on neatly using a palette knife. Top with another biscuit and dip the edges in melted chocolate (see page 6) or icing sugar.

Put the sandwiches on the prepared tray or paper in the freezer as you make them, and leave to firm up for at least 1 hour.

Autumn

Bonfire cracklers

With their crackly tops and hidden chilli 'firework' inside, these biscuits are perfect for bonfire night. The chilli adds a delicious warmth but the biscuits can also be made without it.

MAKES AT LEAST 30

175 g dark chocolate, at
    least 70% cocoa solids
50 g unsalted butter
1 tsp Camp coffee
    essence
100 g hazelnuts, toasted
    (see page 7)
175 g plain flour
¼ tsp salt
1 tsp hot chilli powder, or
    to taste
¼ tsp ground cinnamon
½ tsp baking powder
2 eggs
150 g caster sugar
50 g granulated sugar
50 g icing sugar
icing sugar or cocoa
    powder, to dust

YOU WILL ALSO NEED
Small ice-cream scoop
    (optional)

Put the chocolate, butter and coffee essence in a heatproof bowl over a pan of simmering water. Once the ingredients have melted together, take off the heat and leave to cool a little.

Put the hazelnuts in a food processor or blender with the flour, salt, chilli powder, cinnamon and baking powder and whizz until finely ground. Alternatively, put the nuts in a plastic bag and crush with a rolling pin finely, then mix with the ingredients by hand.

Whisk the eggs and caster sugar in a mixer at a high speed for 5–6 minutes, until the mixture looks pale and mousse-like. Add the cooled melted chocolate and whisk gently until just combined.

Using a large metal spoon, fold the egg mixture into the dry ingredients. Cover with cling film and chill for at least 1 hour, or even overnight.

Preheat the oven to 160°C/Mark 3 and line two baking trays with non-stick baking paper.

Put the granulated sugar in one bowl and the icing sugar in another. Using a small ice-cream scoop or a tablespoon, take pieces of the chilled dough (it will be quite hard) and roll into balls using your hands. Roll each ball first in the granulated sugar, then in the icing sugar and place on the prepared baking trays. I like the biscuits puffed up and round, but if you'd prefer a flatter version, press them down with your hand before putting them in the oven.

Bake for 12–15 minutes, until the tops of the biscuits are cracked. Cool on their trays. Dust with icing sugar or cocoa powder to serve.

Brambly butterscotchers

These are my favourite autumn biscuits. I love blackberry-picking and the long walks when we discover hedgerows bulging with fruit, and clamber into prickly hedges to claim our treasure. The butterscotch biscuits are jewelled with crunchy butter toffee and our plundered blackberry bounty.

MAKES ABOUT 40

60 g unsalted butter, softened

55 g white vegetable fat, such as Flora White

100 g dark brown sugar

300 g granulated sugar

½ tsp vanilla extract

2 eggs

350 g plain flour

1½ tsp bicarbonate of soda

1½ tsp cream of tartar

½ tsp salt

100 g shop-bought chewy toffees, roughly chopped

125 g blackberries, preferably from hedgerows (if only shop-bought are available, choose the smallest, wildest-looking ones)

Preheat the oven to 180°C/Mark 4 and line two baking trays with non-stick baking paper.

Cream the butter, vegetable fat, sugar and vanilla for at least 3 minutes in a mixer, longer by hand. Scrape down the sides of the bowl and beat in the eggs.

Sift in the dry ingredients and mix on a low speed or gently by hand.

Using a metal spoon, very gently fold in the chopped toffees and the blackberries until fairly evenly dispersed. I like to make sure some of the blackberries stay whole as this makes the biscuits look and taste even better. I also like to freeze half the mixture at this point so I can savour the brambly taste of autumn long after the blackberry season is over.

Using two tablespoons, place dollops of the mixture on the prepared baking trays, spacing them at least 3 cm apart. Flatten a little with your fingertips and bake for 15–18 minutes, or until fairly firm and golden. Remove from the oven and use a small palette knife to tidy up any toffee overspills by pushing them back to the edge of the biscuits while still warm. Leave the biscuits to cool on their trays for at least 20 minutes so that the toffee can firm up a bit. They will still be gorgeously chewy.

* *Miranda's Variations*

Add ½ tsp ground cinnamon to the dry ingredients and replace the blackberries with the same amount of chopped fresh figs.

Fat apple rascals

This is my apple version of a traditional biscuit recipe called fat rascals. They're also known as Yorkshire tea biscuits, and my mother, who grew up in Scarborough, remembers them as one of the first things she baked as a child. Simple to make and scone-like in their ingredients and taste, traditional fat rascals have been made since Elizabethan times. I think they taste a bit like apple pie wrapped up in a biscuit – absolutely delicious – and I love them even more dearly because of their name.

MAKES AT LEAST 12
225 g self-raising flour
¼ tsp salt
110 g butter, straight
    from the fridge, finely
    chopped
1oz soft light brown
    sugar
100 g cooking apple,
    chopped into small
    chunks
50 g sultanas
3 tsp milk
golden or white
    granulated sugar, or
    demerara
½ tsp ground cinnamon

Sift the flour and salt into a bowl, then rub in the butter with your fingers or whizz in a food processor. Add the soft light brown sugar, apples, sultanas and milk and mix well.

Bring the dough together with your hands and knead gently. Squash into a flat disc, then place between two sheets of cling film and squash even flatter with your hands. Wrap tightly and chill for about 30 minutes.

Preheat the oven to 180°C/Mark 4 and line two baking trays with non-stick baking paper.

Lightly flour a work surface and roll out the chilled dough as thinly as the apples will allow, about 5–10 mm. Cut into squares using a sharp knife and use a palette knife to lift them carefully onto the prepared trays, spacing them at least 3 cm apart.

Mix the granulated or demerara sugar with the cinnamon and sprinkle generously over the squares. Bake for about 20 minutes, until golden. Set aside to cool on their trays.

Upside-down biscuits

Caramelised and sticky, these biscuits are reminiscent of tarte tatin. I like to make half of them with apple and half with plums, but you can vary the fruit according to what's available. They make an easy pudding served with vanilla ice cream.

MAKES 24

125 g unsalted butter, softened

80 g caster sugar

1 tsp vanilla extract

1 egg

225 g plain flour, sifted

50 g ground almonds

icing sugar, to dust

FOR THE FILLING

150 g unsalted butter, softened

115 g soft light brown sugar

½ tsp vanilla extract

1 medium-sized eating or cooking apple, cored and finely slice

6 plums, preferably small

YOU WILL ALSO NEED

Round cutter, slightly larger than the holes in your baking trays

Cream the butter, sugar and vanilla in a mixer. Scrape down the sides of the bowl and beat in the egg.

On a low speed, mix in the flour and almonds until a dough forms. Shape into a flat disc, wrap in cling film and chill for 1 hour.

Meanwhile, make the filling. Cream the butter, sugar and vanilla until very smooth, then set aside.

Finely slice the apple. Cut the plums in half and discard the stones (large plums should be cut into quarters).

Preheat the oven to 200°C/Mark 6 and place two 12-hole baking trays on the work surface. Cut squares of non-stick baking paper slightly larger than the holes in your trays, scrunch them in your hand, then use them to line the holes. Scrunching the squares makes them fit better, but they don't need to fit perfectly.

Put 1 tablespoon of the butter mixture into each lined hole. Place a layer of apple pieces on top of the mixture in one tray, and put half a plum on top in the other tray.

Place the chilled dough between two sheets of cling film and roll out to a thickness of 3 mm. Lift off the top sheet of cling film and stamp out circles of dough slightly larger than the holes in the baking trays. Press a circle on top of each filled hole and bake for 15–20 minutes, until golden brown. It is worth putting a baking tray in the bottom of your oven to catch any sticky drips.

Cool the biscuits in their trays for about 20 minutes so that the caramel firms up. Use a palette knife to carefully loosen the biscuits and turn them the right way up on a wire rack. Gently peel off the paper while warm. Dust with icing sugar before serving.

Speculoos leaves

Speculoos is a spicy biscuit dough, believed to be Dutch in origin, but very popular in France. These thin, crispy and dark biscuits made from it should really be eaten at a Parisian pavement café on an autumnal weekend. Failing that, I make them with oak leaf- and acorn-shaped cutters to recreate a Parisian atmosphere in my kitchen. They are also stylish cut into oblongs in the traditional French style.

MAKES ABOUT 30

100 g unsalted butter, softened

250 g soft dark brown sugar

1 egg

260 g plain flour

½ tsp baking powder

½ tsp salt

1 tbsp ground cinnamon

1½ tsp ground ginger

½ tsp ground cloves

YOU WILL ALSO NEED

Cutters (whatever shape you like)

Cream the butter and sugar in a mixer for about 2 minutes. Scrape down the sides of the bowl, then beat in the egg at a fast speed until well combined.

Combine the flour, baking powder, salt and spices in a bowl, then sift them onto the egg mixture and stir until a dough forms.

Squash the dough into two flat discs, wrap tightly in cling film and chill for about 1 hour.

Preheat the oven to 180°C/Mark 4 and line two baking trays with non-stick baking paper.

Dust a work surface and rolling pin with flour and roll out the dough to a thickness of 2–3 mm. Using your chosen cutters, stamp out shapes and use a palette knife to transfer them carefully to the prepared baking trays. Recombine the offcuts of dough, then chill a little before rolling out again and stamping out more shapes.

Bake the biscuits for 8–10 minutes, or until the edges start to darken. Set aside to cool on their trays. The biscuits will harden in about 20 minutes.

Hazelnut and chocolate chip crumbles

These are the perfect biscuits for a leaf-kicking kind of autumn day. The ground hazelnuts give them a deep nuttiness, which is enhanced by the toffee-flavoured sugars. I like to spoon the dough in craggy heaps so they look imperfect and irresistibly homemade. They are delicious eaten fresh from the oven, but they need to firm up on their trays for at least five minutes before you devour them.

MAKES AT LEAST 20

170 g unsalted butter, softened

50 g golden caster sugar

50 g muscovado sugar

100 g hazelnuts, toasted (see page 7) and skins rubbed off

200 g plain flour

100 g dark chocolate, at least 70% cocoa solids, chopped

Preheat the oven to 160°C/Mark 3 and line two baking trays with non-stick baking paper.

Cream together the butter and sugars, ideally in a mixer at high speed. Stop after about a minute and scrape down the sides of the bowl, then mix again for another 2–3 minutes.

Whizz 60 g of the hazelnuts in a food processor or blender for about 30 seconds – they should look like breadcrumbs. Add them to the butter mixture along with the flour. Mix well, scraping down the sides of the bowl, until a dough forms.

Roughly chop the remaining 40 g of hazelnuts and use a tablespoon to mix them into the dough along with the chocolate. Spoon craggy heaps of the mixture onto the prepared baking trays and flatten a little with your fingertips. Bake for about 20 minutes, or until golden – the surface of the biscuits should look dry and slightly cracked. Set aside to firm up on their trays for at least 5 minutes before serving.

Cinder toffee biscuits

I love the magic of making a pan full of bubbling honeycomb.
Break leftover honeycomb into chunks and enjoy on its own.

MAKES ABOUT 20

150 g unsalted butter

100 g demerara or
   granulated sugar

1 tbsp golden syrup

1 tbsp milk

1 tsp bicarbonate of soda

240 g plain flour, sifted

100 g good-quality milk
   chocolate, at least 37%
   cocoa solids, chopped,
   plus 100 g extra for
   drizzling

FOR THE TOFFEE

70 g caster sugar

2 tsp golden syrup

1 tsp bicarbonate of soda

Preheat the oven to 180°C/Mark 4 and line two baking trays with non-stick baking paper.

Melt the butter, sugar and syrup in a large pan, stirring all the time. Remove from the heat when it starts to come to the boil.

Combine the milk and bicarbonate of soda in a cup, add to the pan and mix well – the mixture will become pale and frothy.

Put the flour into a separate bowl and pour the melted mixture on top. Stir with a wooden spoon until well combined.

Use your hands to make walnut-sized balls of dough. Flatten them with your palm, then place a few pieces of chocolate in the middle of each circle. Roll back into balls and place on the prepared trays with the seam underneath, spacing them at least 3 cm apart. Flatten a little with your hand again, then bake for 10–15 minutes, until golden. Cool the biscuits on their trays for about 15 minutes, then use a palette knife to transfer them carefully to a wire rack.

Meanwhile, make the cinder toffee. Line a large shallow baking tray with greaseproof paper and put next to the hob.

Put the sugar and syrup into a large pan and bring to the boil. Boil for about 2½ minutes, or until golden in colour. Remove from the heat and stir in the bicarbonate of soda – the mixture will froth and bubble to fill the pan.

Quickly pour the mixture onto the lined baking tray and leave to cool at room temperature until completely hard – about 15 minutes. When cold, break the cinder toffee into small pieces. If you're not going to use it straight away, store it in a tightly sealed container or cellophane bag or it will become soggy.

Melt the chocolate for drizzling (see page 6). Slide baking paper under the wire rack and drizzle the chocolate over the biscuits. Sprinkle with toffee while the chocolate is still wet and leave to set.

Pear and ginger fairings

This recipe is an autumnal twist on the Cornish fairing, a spiced ginger biscuit. 'Fairings' was the name given to edible gifts sold at fairs across Cornwall, and it is thought that men gave them to their sweethearts and children. These fairings are great for munching on walks and lovely with a steaming cup of coffee in the garden.

MAKES AT LEAST 20

225 g plain flour

½ tsp salt

2 tsp baking powder

2 tsp bicarbonate of soda

2 tsp ground mixed spice

2 tsp ground ginger

100 g unsalted butter, straight from the fridge, roughly chopped

10 g crystallised ginger, roughly chopped

110 g caster sugar

4 tbsp golden syrup

75 g dried pear, roughly chopped into small pieces

Preheat the oven to 200°C/Mark 6 and line two baking trays with non-stick baking paper.

If you are making this recipe in a food processor (the easiest way), whizz together the flour, salt, baking powder, bicarbonate of soda, mixed spice and ground ginger. Add the butter and crystallised ginger and whizz again until the mixture resembles coarse breadcrumbs. If you are making the recipe by hand, chop the crystallised ginger as finely as you can and rub the butter into the dry ingredients with your fingertips. Add the sugar and whizz again or stir to combine.

Gently warm the golden syrup in a small pan, add to the mixture and mix until well combined. Finally, stir in the dried pear. The dough should be quite firm and not too sticky.

Using your hands, roll the dough into walnut-sized balls and place them on the prepared baking trays. Flatten a little with the palm of your hand and bake for 5 minutes on the highest shelves in the oven. Swap the trays around and bake for a further 6–7 minutes, until the biscuits look golden and puffy. They will still be soft when you take them out of the oven, so leave them to cool and firm up on their trays.

Toblerone biscuits

Chunks of Toblerone and crunchy toasted almonds create a delicious biscuit that is impossible to resist.

MAKES ABOUT 24

200 g unsalted butter, softened

100 g caster sugar

100 g icing sugar

1 egg plus 1 egg yolk, lightly beaten

1 tsp vanilla extract

300 g plain flour

½ tsp salt

½ tsp baking powder

200 g Toblerone, roughly chopped

150 g almonds, toasted and roughly chopped (see page 7)

YOU WILL ALSO NEED

Small ice-cream scoop (optional)

Preheat the oven to 180°C/Mark 4 and line two baking trays with non-stick baking paper.

Cream the butter and sugars for about 2 minutes, until very light and fluffy. Add the eggs and vanilla extract, and beat well to combine.

Sift in the flour, salt and baking powder, then fold in with a large metal spoon. Finally, fold in the Toblerone and chopped almonds.

Using a small ice-cream scoop or two tablespoons, place dollops of the dough on the prepared baking trays, spacing them at least 3 cm apart. Bake for about 12–15 minutes, or until pale golden and slightly squidgy. Set aside to cool and firm up on their trays.

Winter

Hot chocolate dunkers

Long, slim and designed for dunking, these biscuits will bring delight when enjoyed with the frothiest, creamiest mug of hot chocolate.

MAKES ABOUT 30

60 g hazelnuts, toasted (see page 7)

50 g dark chocolate, at least 70% cocoa solids

225 g unsalted butter, softened and chopped

150 g caster sugar

1 tsp freshly grated nutmeg

½ tsp ground cinnamon

240 g plain flour

100 g white chocolate, for decorating

Preheat the oven to 180°C/Mark 4 and line two baking trays with non-stick baking paper.

Put the hazelnuts and chocolate in a food processor or blender and whizz together until quite fine. Don't worry if there are some biggish lumps – these will give a nice texture to the biscuits.

Combine the nut mixture with the butter, sugar and spices. Add the flour and mix until it comes together as a sticky dough.

Lightly flour your hands and a work surface. Place the dough on it and shape into four similar-sized logs about 3–4 cm in diameter. Place two logs on each prepared tray, spacing them at least 12 cm apart, then use a fork to flatten each log widthways into a rectangle about 8 cm wide and 1 cm thick. Press firmly, dipping the fork into a little water if it starts to stick. There should be at least 10 cm between the flattened rectangles.

Bake for 20–25 minutes, then cut across each rectangle to make fingers about 3 cm wide. Allow to cool on their trays for at least 10 minutes before attempting to transfer them to a wire rack. Leave until completely cold.

Melt the white chocolate (see page 6). Slide a sheet of greaseproof paper under the wire rack, then use a spoon to drizzle the chocolate over two-thirds of each biscuit – you need about a third of the biscuit chocolate-free to hold onto whilst dunking.

Spicy Jaffa biscuits

Warm the cockles of your heart on a wintry day with these spicy biscuits: a spongy base topped with chilli-infused orange marmalade jelly and a thick layer of dark chocolate.

MAKES ABOUT 20

100 g unsalted butter, softened

100 g caster sugar

1 egg, lightly beaten

1 tbsp golden syrup

150 g plain flour

1 tsp bicarbonate of soda

pinch of salt

FOR THE TOPPING

1 x 135 g packet orange jelly

100 ml boiling water

2 tsp chilli marmalade, or 2 tsp shredded orange marmalade mixed with ½ tsp crushed chilli flakes (or to taste)

20 ml freshly squeezed orange juice

200 g dark chocolate, at least 70% cocoa solids, broken into pieces

YOU WILL ALSO NEED

4 cm round metal cutter

To make the filling chop the jelly into small pieces and cover with the boiling water. Mix in the chilli marmalade, stirring well to combine, then stir in the orange juice. Line your smallest shallow baking tray with cling film. Pour in the jelly and put it in the fridge to set. This should take only about 45 minutes

Melt the chocolate (see page 6), then set aside to cool. It needs to be completely cold but still runny before using.

Preheat the oven to 180°C/Mark 4 and line two baking trays with non-stick baking paper.

To make the bases, cream the butter and sugar until smooth. Add the egg and golden syrup and beat again until well combined. Sift in the dry ingredients, then mix with a large metal spoon.

Using a teaspoon, spoon the dough into circles about 4 cm wide onto the prepared trays, spacing them at least 5 cm apart.

Bake for 10 minutes, then swap and rotate the trays to ensure an even bake. Bake for a further 3–5 minutes, or until the biscuits are pale golden with darker edges. Cool on their trays for about 2 minutes, then transfer them to a wire rack and leave until cold.

When the jelly has set, use the cling film to lift it onto a chopping board. Using a round metal cutter slightly smaller than the biscuits, stamp out circles.

Place all the biscuits on a large sheet of non-stick baking paper and use a palette knife to place a circle of jelly on top of each.

Check that the chocolate is cold but still runny – it must not be at all warm otherwise it will melt the jelly. Spoon it on top of the jelly, then carefully smooth it over the top of the biscuits. Leave to harden completely before serving.

Chocolate and stem ginger warmers

With a ginger and sticky chocolate middle, this is a 'hot-water bottle' of a biscuit.

MAKES ABOUT 20

70 g golden syrup

135 g unsalted butter

320 g self-raising flour

40 g cocoa powder

pinch of salt

1 tbsp ground ginger

1 tsp bicarbonate of soda

185 g caster sugar

25 g soft light brown
    sugar

1 egg, lightly beaten

100 g dark chocolate, at
    least 70% cocoa solids,
    for drizzling

FOR THE FILLING

1 ball of stem ginger

60 g dark chocolate, at
    least 70% cocoa solids,
    coarsely grated

20 g golden syrup

YOU WILL ALSO NEED

Garlic press (optional)

Put the syrup and butter into a small pan and heat until they have melted together. Set aside to cool a little.

Sift the flour, cocoa powder, salt, ginger and bicarbonate of soda into a large bowl, add the sugars and mix to combine.

Preheat the oven to 160°C/Mark 3 and line two baking trays with non-stick baking paper.

Pour the melted syrup mixture and the beaten egg into the dry ingredients and mix well. Bring the last bits together with your hands to form a dough.

Now make the filling. Use a garlic press to crush the stem ginger, or finely chop it with a sharp knife. Place in a bowl and stir in the grated chocolate and syrup.

Using your hands, form walnut-sized pieces of dough and make a thumbhole in the top of each one – you might need to flour your thumb to make a clean hole. Squash in about half a teaspoon of filling. Bring the edges of the dough over the filling to cover it, then put the balls, seam-side down, on the prepared trays, spacing them at least 3 cm apart. Flatten a little with your hand before baking for 15–20 minutes – the middles should be slightly sticky.

Set the biscuits aside to cool on their trays for at least 5 minutes, then use a palette knife to transfer them carefully to a wire rack. Leave until completely cold.

If you wish to decorate the biscuits, melt the chocolate (see page 6). Slide a sheet of greaseproof paper under the rack and use a spoon to drizzle the chocolate over the biscuits. Leave the chocolate to set before serving.

Mini Christmas puddings

What could be prettier at Christmas than a plate of tiny puddings?
The dough can be shaped and frozen a month in advance.

MAKES AT LEAST 24

25 g currants

25 g mixed peel

25 g raisins

2 tsp brandy

100 g unsalted butter,
    softened

65 g soft light brown
    sugar

½ tsp vanilla extract

1 tbsp finely grated
    orange zest

1 tbsp finely grated
    lemon zest

2 tsp treacle

1 tsp ground cinnamon

pinch of freshly grated
    nutmeg

25 g flaked almonds,
    toasted (see page 7)

200 g self-raising flour,
    sifted

25 g ground almonds

demerara sugar

100 g white chocolate

holly sprigs made from
    icing, or chopped glacé
    cherries

Put the currants, mixed peel and raisins in a bowl with the
brandy. Stir, cover with cling film and put in the fridge to steep for
anything from 1 hour to a week. When you're ready to use it, strain
off any remaining liquid, then finely chop the fruit or whizz in a
food processor.

Preheat the oven to 200°C/Mark 6 and line two baking trays
with non-stick baking paper.

Cream the butter, sugar, vanilla and zests. Warm the treacle in
the microwave for 10 seconds on High and add to the butter mixture
along with the spices. Mix well to combine.

Roughly crush the toasted almonds with your hands and add
to the butter mixture along with the flour, ground almonds and
chopped fruit. Mix well to combine.

Roll the mixture into walnut-sized balls with your hands, then
roll each ball in the demerara sugar and place on the prepared
trays, spacing them at least 2 cm apart. Bake for 10–15 minutes,
until the biscuits look dry and slightly cracked on the surface. Set
aside to cool on their trays for about 5 minutes, then use a palette
knife to transfer them to a wire rack.

While the biscuits are cooling, melt the chocolate (see page 6),
stirring regularly. Slide a sheet of greaseproof paper under the
rack and spoon about a teaspoonful of chocolate onto each of the
biscuits, letting it run down the sides. Allow it to set a little, but
while it is still sticky, press some pretty decorations onto the top. I
like to use holly sprigs made from sugar florist paste (see page 13),
Christmas sprinkles or finely chopped glacé cherries. Allow the
chocolate to set completely before serving.

Snowballs

When the snow lies thick on the ground, our kitchen is renamed the Snow Café, a place for exhausted snowballers to refuel before the next round commences. The menu requires appropriate snowy treats, and these snowballs are just the thing. They would also look beautiful at a wintry tea party or served as petit fours on a glass cake-stand dusted with fresh (icing sugar) snow.

MAKES ABOUT 20

100 g unsalted butter, softened

140 g icing sugar, sifted

½ tsp vanilla extract

110 g plain flour, sifted

25 g cornflour, sifted

35 g desiccated coconut

YOU WILL ALSO NEED

Small ice-cream scoop (optional)

Preheat the oven to 180°C/Mark 4 and line two baking trays with non-stick baking paper.

Put the butter in a bowl, add 40 g of the icing sugar and beat for 2 minutes, ideally in a mixer, until light and fluffy. Add the vanilla and mix again. Mix in the flour and cornflour, then gently stir in the coconut.

Using a small ice-cream scoop or your hands, form the dough into walnut-sized balls. Place them on the prepared trays, spacing them at least 3 cm apart, and bake for about 15 minutes, until firm to touch.

Take the biscuits out of the oven and, taking care not to burn yourself, drop them one at a time into a bowl of the remaining icing sugar. Roll them around to cover, then lift out and place on a sheet of non-stick baking paper. Leave to cool completely. Before serving, dredge with more icing sugar using a shaker or sieve to make them look like freshly made snowballs.

Fireside biscuits

These are reassuring biscuits to enjoy snuggled up in front of the fire – perfect with a glass of milk and slippers.

MAKES ABOUT 20

150 g unsalted butter, softened

150 g soft light brown sugar

1 egg, lightly beaten

1 tsp vanilla extract

80 g plain flour, sifted

pinch of salt

25 g cocoa powder, sifted

1 tsp ground cinnamon

1 tsp baking powder

185 g porridge oats

150 g milk chocolate, roughly chopped

YOU WILL ALSO NEED

Small ice-cream scoop (optional)

Preheat the oven to 180°C/Mark 4 and line two baking trays with non-stick baking paper.

Cream together the butter and sugar for about 2 minutes. Scrape down the sides of the bowl, add the egg and vanilla and beat again.

Sift in the flour, salt, cocoa powder, cinnamon and baking powder, then tip in the oats. Mix gently until just combined, then use a large metal spoon to fold in the chocolate.

Using a small ice-cream scoop or two tablespoons, place dollops of the dough on the prepared trays, spacing them at least 3 cm apart. Flatten with the palm of your hand, then bake for about 15 minutes, until golden and dryish on top. Set aside on their trays to cool for 10 minutes, then use a palette knife to transfer them carefully to a wire rack to firm up.

Boozy white chocolate and cranberry cookies

Soaking the cranberries in port adds a sweet richness and sophistication to these biscuits. They're perfect for Christmas and wonderfully handy, as they can be made in advance and frozen before the flurry of Christmas baking commences.

MAKES ABOUT 30

125 g dried cranberries, roughly chopped

120 ml port

75 g unsalted butter, softened

150 g granulated sugar

125 g soft light brown sugar

½ tsp vanilla extract

1 egg, lightly beaten

100 g white chocolate, at least 25% cocoa solids

½ tsp bicarbonate of soda

150 g plain flour

125 g white chocolate chunks

YOU WILL ALSO NEED

Small ice-cream scoop (optional)

Put the cranberries and port into a small bowl, stir and cover with cling film. Place in the fridge to steep for at least 1 hour or overnight.

Preheat the oven to 180°C/Mark 4 and line two baking trays with non-stick baking paper.

Cream the butter, sugars and vanilla until light and fluffy. Add the egg to the mixture and beat well to combine.

Drain the cranberries through a sieve, reserving the port. Add 1½ teaspoons of the port to the butter mixture and stir in with a metal spoon.

Melt the 100 g of chocolate (see page 6), stirring carefully as it melts, then fold it into the butter mixture using a metal spoon. Sift in the dry ingredients and fold in gently. Finally, fold in the drained cranberries and chocolate chunks.

Using a small ice-cream scoop or two tablespoons, place dollops of the dough on the prepared trays, spacing them at least 4 cm apart. Bake for about 12 minutes, until pale golden around the edges and a little runny in the centre. The biscuits will firm up as they set but still have soft squidgy middles.

Allow the biscuits to cool on their trays for at least 10 minutes before attempting to move them. Use a palette knife to transfer them carefully to a wire rack to cool completely, or eat them warm.

Festive florentines

My friend and florentine fanatic Jo has tested the world's best florentines and assures me that this recipe hits the spot. Chewy, with the perfect balance of fruit and nuts, these are delicious and stylish.

MAKES ABOUT 24

80 g candied peel

50 g raisins

30 g cranberries

30 g flaked almonds

80 g walnuts or pecans, chopped

25 g crystallised ginger, roughly chopped (optional)

50 g plain flour, sifted

50 g unsalted butter

150 g light muscovado sugar

100 ml double cream

60 ml clear honey

FOR THE TOPPING

300 g dark chocolate, at least 70% cocoa solids, or a mixture of toppings, such as 100 g white chocolate plus ¼ tsp freshly grated nutmeg, 100 g milk chocolate plus ¼ tsp mixed spice

Preheat the oven to 160°C/Mark 3 and line two large baking trays with non-stick baking paper.

Place the peel, raisins, cranberries, nuts and crystallised ginger (if using) in a bowl with the flour and stir to combine.

Put the butter, sugar, cream and honey in a medium pan. Bring to the boil and boil for 7 minutes, stirring constantly – do not let the mixture caramelise. Remove from the heat and stir in the dry mixture to make a sticky but spoonable dough.

Place ½ teaspoons of the mixture on the prepared trays, spacing them at least 5 cm apart as the mixture spreads a lot. Bake for 12 minutes, or until golden. Tidy the edges with a palette knife while the biscuits are still warm, then leave them to cool and harden on their trays for about 10 minutes. Use a palette knife to transfer them carefully to a wire rack and cool completely.

Choose the topping(s) you prefer and melt each type of chocolate and its flavouring in separate bowls (see page 6). When melted, stir well.

Slide a sheet of greaseproof paper under the wire rack, then turn the florentines over so they are upside down. Use a palette knife to spread a thin layer of chocolate over the base of each biscuit. Set aside for about 15 minutes, until starting to set, then use a fork to make wavy lines in the chocolate. Allow to set completely.

These florentines will keep for up to a week in an airtight container.

BISCUIT DECORATIONS

It is lovely to make biscuits as decorations to hang on a Christmas tree, or for a pretty Easter display hung on branches of pussy willow or blossom. You can use any of the doughs in chapter 9 (see pages 182–183), but the gingerbread will last the longest. You will need to make a hole in the biscuits as soon as they come out of the oven. Use a wooden skewer to make the hole about 1 cm from the top edge, wiggling it a little to make it clean and slightly larger than the skewer. Leave to cool before decorating.

Decorate the biscuits with simple piped royal icing or use the flooding technique as described in chapter 9. Once the icing is completely set, use a darning needle to thread a length of ribbon through each biscuit, or poke the ribbon through the hole using a cocktail stick.

4 OUTDOOR BISCUITS

Biscuits are perfect for walks, for days out and, above all, for adventures. Outdoor biscuits need to be wholesome – many of them are packed with brown sugar and oats to give much-needed energy – and fairly sturdy because they are designed to be wrapped tightly in foil and snuggled into a pocket, but they will also sit happily in a picnic basket with your flask and other provisions.

There is something special about eating outdoors, and many of the biscuits in this book could be enjoyed on trips to the beach or on wintry sledging escapades. This chapter contains the biscuits that I most often make to take out with my family. We love being outdoors, and whether I am providing supplies for pirates in the tree-house or snacks to be enjoyed while sitting on a windy headland after a bracing walk on the beach, the recipes that follow seem to hit the spot – a chance to stop and be together and share a biscuity adventure.

Biscuits for adventures

These are probably the homemade biscuits I loved most when I was little; our great family friend Jean made them all the time. We always had wonderful adventures with her children on our holidays together, with our camper vans, boats and tents. Just a bite of one of these biscuits brings all those wonderful childhood memories rushing back.

MAKES AT LEAST 18

85 g desiccated coconut

85 g rolled oats

100 g plain flour

100 g caster sugar

100 g unsalted butter

1 heaped tbsp golden
    syrup

1 tsp bicarbonate of soda

2 tbsp boiling water

Preheat the oven to 180°C/Mark 4 and line two baking trays with non-stick baking paper.

Mix the coconut, oats, flour and caster sugar in a bowl.

Melt the butter in a pan, then add the golden syrup. Put the bicarbonate of soda in a cup, add the boiling water, then pour this into the butter mixture. It will froth and increase in volume. Add to the dry ingredients and stir gently.

Put heaped teaspoonfuls of the mixture onto the prepared baking trays, placing them at least 5 cm apart. Bake for 10–12 minutes, until golden. Set aside to firm up on their trays for about 5 minutes, then use a palette knife to transfer them carefully to a wire rack. These biscuits will keep for a week in an airtight container.

Coat-pocket biscuits

I have become notorious among family and friends for having these biscuits with me at all times. I found that with children and a hungry husband, walks or outings were often cut short or spoilt by hungry tummies. They are a wonderful 'pocketful of quiet' during important occasions, such as weddings or school concerts, and are helpful distractions when visiting the doctor.

MAKES ABOUT 80

250 g unsalted butter, softened

140 g icing sugar

1 egg yolk

½ tsp vanilla extract (optional)

250 g plain flour

50 g cornflour

50 g currants or finely chopped sultanas or raisins

100 g chocolate chips or grated chocolate

YOU WILL ALSO NEED

2 cm metal cutter, or small metal bottle top of similar size (optional)

Cream the butter and sugar. Beat the egg yolk with the vanilla (if using) and slowly add to the mixture, stirring until well combined.

Add the flour and cornflour and mix until a dough starts to form. Finally, add the chocolate chips and currants, stirring to incorporate evenly, or bring the mixture together with your hands and knead gently. Split the dough in half, shape each piece into a ball, then squash each ball into a flat disc shape. Wrap each disc tightly in cling film and chill for about 30 minutes.

Preheat the oven to 180°C/Mark 4 and line two baking trays with non-stick baking paper.

Place each disc of chilled dough between two large sheets of cling film and roll out as thinly as the chocolate chips will allow. Peel off the top sheet of cling film and use your chosen cutter to stamp out lots of shapes. (Note that it is easier to stamp them all out and lift them off afterwards.) You might need to dip the bottle top in flour to stop the dough sticking to it. Use the flat of your hand to hit the top and the dough should come away cleanly. (If you don't have a suitable cutter to hand, roll tiny balls of dough smaller than a cherry and flatten them with a palette knife.)

Using a palette knife, lift several dough shapes at a time off the cling film and place them on the prepared trays, spacing them at least 3 cm apart. Bake for 10 minutes, until lightly golden. Set aside to cool on their trays before removing with a palette knife.

Sledging biscuits

These are great biscuits to give everyone some much-needed energy when out sledging, and would also be perfect for taking on a bracing walk in wintry weather. They are packed with oats, raisins and chocolate chips for extra sustenance, helping to keep the cold at bay, giving a burst of energy for the final sledge-pull uphill, and encouraging little walkers to make it home without a carry. They're also scrummy with a steaming mug of hot chocolate when you get back indoors. This recipe makes a big batch of biscuits, but they keep well if stored in an airtight container.

MAKES ABOUT 30

270 g unsalted butter,
    softened
160 g caster sugar
160 g demerara sugar
2 eggs
1 tsp vanilla extract
380 g plain flour
½ tsp salt
1 tsp bicarbonate of soda
100 g jumbo oats
120 g raisins
150 g chocolate chunks
    or chips (I used 100 g
    milk chocolate and
    50 g dark chocolate)

Preheat the oven to 180°C/Mark 4 and line two baking trays with non-stick baking paper.

Cream the butter and sugars until pale and fluffy. Add the eggs and vanilla and mix again until well combined.

Sift the flour, salt and bicarbonate of soda into a large bowl, add the oats and stir to combine. Add to the butter mixture and mix until a dough starts to form. At that point, add the chocolate and raisins and mix just a little more.

Using your hands, roll the dough into balls the size of a golf ball. Place on the prepared baking trays, spacing them at least 5 cm apart, and flatten a little with the palm of your hand. Bake for about 10 minutes, or until golden brown, dry and fairly firm – keep an eye on them as they can suddenly burn underneath and be too crunchy.

Set aside to cool a little on their trays, then, if you can wait, transfer them to a wire rack to cool completely.

Honey biscuits

These are quick and easy to make, and even when provisions are low, you are bound to have the ingredients in the cupboard. Golden, crunchy and tasting of honey, these are great biscuits for adventures, and come with us on lots of walks at the beach and in the woods. You will have them made while everyone else is still finding their wellies and getting ready to go.

MAKES AT LEAST 18

2 heaped tbsp honey

1 tbsp milk

1 tsp bicarbonate of soda

100 g unsalted butter, softened

75 g soft light brown sugar

175 g plain flour, sifted

Preheat the oven to 180°C/Mark 4 and line two baking trays with non-stick baking paper.

Put the honey and milk into a small microwaveable bowl and warm in the microwave on High for 30 seconds. Alternatively, place them in a small pan and warm gently on the hob, stirring all the time. When piping hot, add the bicarbonate of soda and whisk with a fork until frothy.

Cream together the butter and sugar, add the honey mixture and beat again. Finally, add the flour and mix until just combined.

Using your hands, roll the dough into walnut-sized balls and place on the prepared baking trays, spacing them at least 5 cm apart. Flatten them a little with your hand, then bake for about 10 minutes, or until domed and golden. Set aside to cool and firm up on their trays for about 10 minutes, then use a palette knife to transfer them carefully to a wire rack. Wait until they are completely cold before wrapping in foil to take on your outings.

Sea salt caramel sprays

Perfect for taking with a picnic to the beach, or to give that sea saltiness of beach-time fun on adventures closer to home. I love the salty caramel taste to these biscuits, but if you prefer more of a toffee flapjack flavour, they are equally delicious with the salt left out. Cover with a thick layer of good-quality dark chocolate for a more indulgent treat, but avoid this on hot days!

MAKES ABOUT 18

240 g unsalted butter

100 g soft light brown sugar

80 g demerara sugar

1 tsp bicarbonate of soda mixed with 1 tbsp boiling water

½ tsp coarse sea salt flakes

100 g plain flour

300 g rolled oats

100 g dark chocolate chips

100 g dark chocolate, for coating (optional)

YOU WILL ALSO NEED

small ice-cream scoop (optional)

Put the butter and sugars in a large pan and stir until melted. Remove from the heat and immediately add the bicarbonate of soda mixture, whisking with a balloon whisk until pale and fluffy.

Add the sea salt, flour and oats and stir to combine. Tip the mixture into a bowl and chill for about 30 minutes.

Preheat the oven to 180°C/Mark 4. Line two baking trays with non-stick baking paper or grease two silicone muffin trays.

Stir the chocolate chips into the chilled mixture. Using a small ice-cream scoop or two tablespoons, place dollops of the mixture on the prepared trays, spacing them at least 5 cm apart. In fact, I prefer to put them into the holes in the muffin trays as this gives a thicker biscuit, almost like a round piece of flapjack.

Bake for 10–15 minutes, or until golden brown. Set aside, without attempting to lift the biscuits, until completely cold. They are then easy to lift with a palette knife or to pop out of the silicone trays.

Smores

If you haven't yet been lucky enough to experience smores, it is time to sample this delicious outdoor indulgence. These melted marshmallow sandwiches taste wonderful and can be made using any firm biscuits. My children make them on the bonfire, and they are also easy to prepare on the glowing embers at the end of a barbecue, so they are a perfect sweet something after a fireworks party or garden supper.

MAKES 12

12 large pink or white
marshmallows (or
24 if you are feeling
super-indulgent and
want to create an extra
mallowy middle)

1 quantity firm biscuit
dough (see pages 28,
154 and 182–183)

100 g dark, milk or white
chocolate (optional)

about 6 tbsp good-quality
jam or chocolate
spread (optional)

YOU WILL ALSO NEED

4 cm round cutter

12 long sharpened sticks
or skewers

1 glowing bonfire or
barbecue

Make the biscuits in advance according to the instructions for your chosen dough. I recommend using a round cutter about 4 cm in diameter. Once baked, set aside until cold.

If you want to make chocolate smores, melt the chocolate (see page 6) and use a palette knife to spread some over the top of each biscuit. (It does not need to look neat or perfectly smooth, as it will melt again later when the sandwiching is done.) Leave to cool and harden.

If you want to make jammy smores, spread the top of each biscuit with a good layer of jam, but do this just before serving. I tend to take a little plastic pot of jam with me to do this stage at the last minute by the fire or barbecue. You could use chocolate spread instead of jam if you prefer.

Put all your prepared biscuits into an airtight container, ready to take to the barbecue or fireworks party.

To make the smores, push a marshmallow onto the end of a sharpened stick or skewer. Hold it over the glowing embers of the bonfire or barbecue and rotate gently until the marshmallow starts to melt. Place it on top of a chocolate- or jam-covered biscuit and sandwich with another biscuit, covered side next to marshmallow. Squeeze together. Repeat until all the biscuits are filled with marshmallows.

5 SAVOURY NIBBLES

Savoury biscuits are great to serve with drinks, either to be nibbled just as they are or as a base for canapés, and are the perfect accompaniment to soups, starters and cheeses. So often overlooked, homemade savoury biscuits can be just as delicious as their sweeter cousins, and their flavours are so much fresher and distinct than shop-bought ones. They can also be made for less than their deli or farm shop counterparts.

This chapter is a collection of my favourite biscuits, a medley of moreish morsels that is bound to get you hooked on savoury biscuits.

Cheese and pickle smackerels

We are pickle-crazy in our house, rarely consuming cheese without an appropriate chutney or pickle on the side. This 'smackerel' of deliciousness is the lazy version for fellow fanatics to enjoy.

MAKES ABOUT 30

50 g unsalted butter, at
   room temperature,
   roughly chopped
100 g plain flour
50 g wholewheat
   semolina
50 g porridge oats
4 tbsp pickle or chutney,
   finely chopped
100 g mature Cheddar
   cheese, grated

YOU WILL ALSO NEED

4 cm round cutter
   (optional)
Pizza wheel (optional)

Put all the ingredients in a food processor and whizz until a dough starts to form. Alternatively, rub the butter into the flour using your fingertips, add the semolina and oats, then stir in the pickle and cheese. Bring the dough together with your hands and knead gently. Divide in half and flatten into two discs. Wrap tightly in cling film and chill for at least 30 minutes.

Preheat the oven to 180°C/Mark 4 and line two baking trays with non-stick baking paper.

Place each disc of chilled dough between two sheets of cling film and roll out to a thickness of roughly 3 mm. Stamp out shapes using your cutter, or cut into squares using a pizza wheel or sharp knife. Transfer to the prepared trays, spacing them at least 3 cm apart. Prick well with a fork and bake for 15–20 minutes, until golden. Allow the biscuits to cool on their trays for at least 10 minutes, then use a palette knife to transfer them carefully to a wire rack to cool completely.

Marmite morsels

You will almost certainly love these biscuits – little parcels tasting of butter, cheese and Marmite. These tempting morsels are perfect for when you need a little something at any time of the day. They're also fabulous to serve with drinks, and ideal for children's lunch boxes.

MAKES ABOUT 30

150 g plain flour

50 g wholemeal flour

150 g mature Cheddar cheese, coarsely grated

1½ tbsp Marmite (more if you are an addict)

150 g unsalted butter, straight from the fridge

1 whole egg plus 1 egg yolk

Put both the flours and cheese into a mixing bowl and stir to combine. Grate in the butter and rub together with your fingertips until the mixture resembles breadcrumbs, or transfer to a food processor and whizz.

Put the Marmite in a small microwaveable bowl or cup and warm in the microwave on High for 10 seconds. Beat in the eggs, then add to the flour mixture, making sure you scrape in all the sticky Marmite. Whizz again or stir with a knife until a dough starts to form. Bring the dough together with your hands and knead gently, then roll into two logs about 3 cm in diameter. Wrap each log tightly in cling film and chill for at least 1 hour (or freeze for future use).

Preheat the oven to 200°C/Mark 6 and line two baking trays with non-stick baking paper.

Using a sharp knife, slice the dough as thinly as possible – ideally, about 3 mm thick, as this will give you wonderful crispy biscuits. Place on the prepared trays, spacing them about 2 cm apart, and bake for 8–10 minutes, or until golden brown and looking quite crispy. Set aside to cool on their trays for at least 5 minutes, then use a palette knife to transfer them to a wire rack to cool completely.

Stilton and walnut nibbles

The combination of walnuts and Stilton in these biscuits is sublime, and they literally melt in the mouth. The dough freezes well, so make a big batch and conjure up biscuits at the drop of a hat to impress unexpected guests.

MAKES ABOUT 60

200 g plain flour, sifted

½ tsp dried mustard powder

generous pinch of salt

freshly ground black pepper

50 g mature Cheddar or Parmesan cheese, roughly grated

150 g Stilton cheese, roughly grated

200 g unsalted butter, straight from the fridge

100 g walnuts, roughly crushed

Put the flour into a bowl and add the mustard powder, salt and some black pepper. Add the cheeses, reserving about 25 g of the Stilton for later. Grate in the butter and add all but 1 tablespoon of the walnuts. Rub the butter into the mixture using your fingertips, or pulse in a food processor. The mixture will quickly form a dough.

Lightly flour a work surface and roll the dough into two logs about 3 cm in diameter. Wrap each log tightly in cling film and chill for at least 1 hour. (If you want to freeze some of the dough at this stage, wrap it in greaseproof paper as well as cling film and tie at each end with string.)

Preheat the oven to 180ºC/Mark 4 and line two baking trays with non-stick baking paper.

Using a sharp knife, cut the chilled dough into slices about 5 mm thick – they should look about the thickness of a £1 coin. Place the discs on the prepared trays, spacing them about 3 cm apart, then sprinkle some of the remaining Stilton and walnut pieces on top of each one. Bake for about 10 minutes, or until pale golden.

As soon as the biscuits come out of the oven, use a large palette knife to transfer them carefully to a wire rack to cool a little. They are wonderful eaten warm the day you bake them, but keep brilliantly in an airtight container. If serving them as a nibble with drinks, they can be perked up by a 2-minute blast in a hot oven.

Pesto and pine nut pieces

Although there's a tiny invasion from Britain in the form of the Cheddar, these creamy yet crunchy nibbles are essentially a taste of Italy. They'd be perfect for accompanying drinks or a starter at a dinner party, especially if you've chosen an Italian-themed menu.

MAKES ABOUT 24

175 g unsalted butter, softened and cut into chunks

75 g Cheddar cheese, grated

100 g Parmesan cheese, grated

2 heaped tbsp good-quality pesto

1 small garlic clove, crushed

175 g plain flour

150 g pine nuts

handful of fresh basil, roughly chopped

Mix the butter with the cheeses, pesto and garlic until smooth and creamy. Add the flour and mix until a sticky dough forms. Stir in the pine nuts and basil with a wooden spoon.

Scrape half the dough onto a sheet of cling film and roll into a log about 4 cm in diameter. Repeat with the remaining dough, then chill both logs for about 30 minutes. If you want to save some dough for future use, it could also be frozen at this point.

Preheat the oven to 180°C/Mark 4 and line two baking trays with non-stick baking paper.

Using a sharp knife, cut the chilled logs into slices about 5 mm thick. Place the discs on the prepared trays, spacing them at least 3 cm apart. Bake for 20 minutes, or until golden and dry on the surface. Set aside on their trays for about 10 minutes, then use a palette knife to transfer them carefully to a wire rack to cool completely.

Sundried tomato spirals

Bursting with the colour and taste of sun-dried tomatoes, these biscuits radiate summer, sunshine and holidays.

MAKES ABOUT 20

150 g plain flour

pinch of salt

50 g Parmesan cheese, grated

100 g unsalted butter, softened

1 egg, separated

1 tbsp sun-dried tomato paste

poppy seeds, for rolling

FOR THE FILLING

75 g sun-dried tomatoes, squeezed to remove excess oil and finely chopped

1 tsp sun-dried tomato paste

Put the flour, salt, Parmesan and butter into a large mixing bowl. Add the egg yolk and tomato paste. Whizz or mix until a dough forms. Bring the dough together with your hands to make a fat log. Place it between two sheets of cling film and gently roll it into a rectangle about 5 mm thick. Remove the top sheet of cling film.

To make the filling, mix the tomatoes with the tomato paste. Spread this mixture all over the dough. With the long edge nearest you, use the bottom sheet of cling film to roll the dough into a long, thin log. Wrap it tightly in the cling film and smooth it into an even shape. Chill for 2 hours. If you want to save the dough for future use, it could be frozen at this point.

Preheat the oven to 200°C/Mark 6 and line two baking trays with non-stick baking paper.

Unwrap the chilled log, brush with the egg white, then roll in the poppy seeds. Cut the log into slices about 5 mm thick and place on the prepared trays, spacing them at least 3 cm apart. Bake for about 15–20 minutes, or until golden. Set the biscuits aside to cool on their trays for at least 10 minutes, then use a palette knife to transfer them carefully to a wire rack to cool completely.

Pumpkin seed and spelt and sesame thins

Crisp, light and splendidly snappy, these thins are crammed full of healthy seeds, wholesome yoghurt and nourishing spelt. They make a tasty snack at any time of the day, a stunning addition to a cheeseboard and a perfect partner for dips.

MAKES ABOUT 48

125 g plain flour

225 g spelt flour

2 tsp baking powder

1½ tsp salt

85 g unsalted butter, at
     room temperature,
     roughly chopped

200 g natural low-fat
     yoghurt

50 g sesame seeds

50 g pumpkin seeds

FOR THE GLAZE

1 egg

1 tbsp clear honey

½ tbsp dark soy sauce

FOR THE TOPPING

25 g sesame seeds

25 g pumpkin seeds

Put the flours, baking powder and salt in a food processor (ideally), or otherwise in a large mixing bowl, and whizz or stir to combine.

Add the butter and pulse or rub in until the mixture resembles breadcrumbs. Add the yoghurt and seeds and mix together until a dough starts to form. Bring it together with your hands, then divide it into four pieces. Wrap each piece tightly in cling film and chill for at least 15 minutes.

Preheat the oven to 200°C/Mark 6 and line two baking trays with non-stick baking paper.

Prepare the glaze by mixing all the ingredients. Put to one side.

Divide one piece of chilled dough into roughly 12 balls and roll each one into a log shape. Lightly flour a work surface and place one log on it. Cover with a sheet of baking parchment, then roll the dough out as thinly as possible. Transfer the small rectangle to one of the prepared trays. Repeat this step until all the dough is used up. The rectangles should be spaced about 3 cm apart.

Generously brush the glaze over each of the rectangles, then sprinkle liberally with the seeds, pressing them into the dough with the back of a spoon. Bake for 20 minutes, or until the biscuits are crisp and golden brown. Use a palette knife to transfer them carefully to wire racks to cool.

These biscuits will store well in an airtight container for about a week. If you want to crisp them up before serving, pop them into a hot oven for 5 minutes.

Honey oatcakes

I make these oatcakes with Manuka honey, which tastes intense and makes a healthy biscuit feel even healthier, but for everyday nibbling you can simply use whatever honey you have in the cupboard. These oatcakes are a sturdy base for canapés, great on a cheeseboard, and work well as 'power' snacks.

MAKES AT LEAST 16

3 tbsp clear honey

1 tbsp boiling water

125 g plain wholemeal flour

50 g plain white flour

200 g medium oatmeal, plus extra for sprinkling

½ tsp sea salt flakes

½ tsp baking powder

100 g unsalted butter, straight from the fridge, chopped into small pieces

25 g lard or white fat, chopped into small pieces

milk, for brushing

YOU WILL ALSO NEED

5 cm round cutter

Measure the honey into a cup and mix with the boiling water. Set aside to cool.

Put all the remaining ingredients except the milk into a food processer or large mixing bowl. Add the honey mixture and whizz or stir until a dough forms. Bring it together with your hands and knead gently to make a smooth ball. Flatten the dough into a disc, wrap tightly in cling film and chill for at least 1 hour.

Preheat the oven to 180°C/Mark 4 and line two baking trays with non-stick baking paper.

Place a sheet of cling film on a work surface, sprinkle with oatmeal and place the chilled dough on it. Cover with another sheet of cling film and roll out to a thickness of 3 mm. Using your cutter, stamp out circles and place them on the prepared trays, spacing them at least 3 cm apart. Prick well with a fork and brush with milk. Bake for 15–20 minutes, until golden. Set aside to cool on their trays.

✳ Miranda's Variations

For canapés, make tiny oatcakes about 3 cm wide and top with Stilton and pear, or mature Cheddar cheese and chutney, or smoked salmon with cream cheese.

For ginger and honey oatcakes, add 1 tsp ground ginger or 1 tsp finely chopped stem ginger to the dry ingredients.

Seriously seedy biscuits

These seedy, digestive-style biscuits are munchy and slightly crunchy, but have a hint of sweetness too. Wonderful on their own, they also go well with cheese.

MAKES ABOUT 16

75 g plain flour

1 tsp baking powder

½ tsp sea salt

75 g wholemeal flour

50 g rolled oats

2 tbsp soft brown sugar

85 g mixed grains and seeds (roughly 20 g each of oats, millet, sunflower seeds and wheatgerm)

100 g unsalted butter, at room temperature

3 tbsp milk

YOU WILL ALSO NEED

4–5 cm round fluted cutter

Sift the plain flour, baking powder and salt into a large bowl. Add the wholemeal flour, oats, sugar and seed mixture and stir with a wooden spoon until everything is evenly combined.

Chop the butter and rub it into the dry ingredients using your fingertips, or whizz in a food processor, until the mixture resembles breadcrumbs. Add the milk and mix with a knife or whizz again until a dough begins to form. Bring it together with your hands and knead gently, then flatten into a disc shape. Wrap tightly in cling film and chill for about 30 minutes.

Preheat the oven to 180°C/Mark 4 and line two baking trays with non-stick baking paper.

Place the chilled dough on a lightly floured surface and roll out to a thickness of 3 mm. Using your cutter, stamp out circles and place them on the prepared trays, spacing them about 2 cm apart. Bake for about 20 minutes, or until golden and a biscuit lifts up easily. Peek underneath to make sure the base looks dry, firm and mottled. Set the biscuits aside to cool and firm up on their trays for about 5 minutes, then use a palette knife to transfer them carefully to a wire rack to cool completely.

Fig biscotti

I adore baking with figs, and love combining them with honey and cheese, so these biscotti are winners. Fantastic on their own or as canapé bases, and great with salads and starters, these stunning little biscuits won't let you down.

MAKES ABOUT 30

2 eggs

2 tbsp clear honey

100 ml olive oil

265 g plain flour

20 g cornflour

2 tsp baking powder

½ tsp salt

½ tsp freshly ground
   black pepper

150 g Parmesan cheese,
   finely grated

175 g dried figs, roughly
   chopped

Line a baking tray with non-stick baking paper.

In a large bowl, whisk together the eggs and honey. Add the olive oil and whisk again. Sift in the flour, cornflour, baking powder and salt, then add the pepper. Stir until all the ingredients are well combined. Add the Parmesan and chopped figs and mix again until a dough forms.

Tip the dough onto a lightly floured work surface and divide in half. Shape each piece into a log about 5 cm in diameter and place on the prepared tray about 5 cm apart. Flatten the logs gently with your hand so they're about 7 cm wide, then cover with cling film and chill for at least 30 minutes.

Preheat the oven to 160°C/Mark 3. Bake the logs for 35 minutes, or until golden and firm. Set aside to cool on their trays for a few minutes, then use the baking paper to transfer them to a chopping board. Use a bread knife to cut each log into slices about 1 cm thick. Arrange the slices flat-side down on the baking tray and return to the oven for about another 15 minutes, until they look golden and dry. Turn the slices over and return to the oven for another 10–15 minutes. The biscuits should be firm, golden and dry. If they are crumbly and scone-like, they need longer in the oven. When ready, set aside to cool on their trays.

*Miranda's Variations

To create a wonderful canapé or starter, top the biscotti with creamy goats' cheese, a sliver of Parma ham and some chopped fresh fig.

To make apricot and walnut biscotti, replace the figs with 100 g organic dried apricots and 75 g chopped walnuts.

Parmesan hearts

These biscuits are light, gorgeously cheesy and meltingly delicious. They look highly refined, suggesting a great deal of effort has gone into their making, but they are in fact incredibly simple to make.

MAKES AT LEAST 24

100 g plain flour

cayenne pepper

25 g semolina

100 g unsalted butter,
    straight from the
    fridge

100 g Parmesan cheese,
    finely grated

2 egg yolks

1 tsp olive oil

1 tbsp milk

1 tbsp mixed seeds
    (optional)

YOU WILL ALSO NEED

Small heart-shaped
    cutter (about 4 cm)

Sift the flour and a pinch of cayenne pepper into a large mixing bowl and stir in the semolina. Coarsely grate the butter into the bowl, then rub it in using your fingertips, or whizz in a food processor, until the mixture resembles breadcrumbs. Stir in 75 g of the Parmesan using a metal spoon.

Put one egg yolk and the olive oil into a cup or small bowl and beat together. Add to the dry ingredients a little at a time, stirring with a knife or pulsing in the food processor. Bring the dough together with your hands to form a flat disc. Wrap tightly in cling film and chill for at least 30 minutes.

Preheat the oven to 180°C/Mark 4 and line two baking trays with non-stick baking paper.

Lightly flour a work surface and roll out the chilled dough to a thickness of about 3 mm. Using your cutter, stamp out heart shapes. Place them on the prepared baking trays, spacing them about 3 cm apart.

Beat the remaining egg yolk with the milk and brush over the top of each biscuit. Sprinkle with the remaining Parmesan, a few seeds (if using) and a dusting of cayenne pepper. Bake for 8–10 minutes, until golden.

*Miranda's Variations

To make a less expensive version of this biscuit, which is also suitable for children, replace the Parmesan with mature Cheddar cheese and omit the cayenne pepper.

6 ALMOST HEALTHY BISCUITS

The recipes in this chapter show that even biscuits can be healthy in their own way. Some are packed full of superfoods, such as berries, and others are appealing because they do not contain dairy ingredients or gluten. My 'free-from' biscuits can appeal to everyone, and show that even if you suffer from intolerances, you can still enjoy delicious biscuits. In fact, they taste so good that no one will guess they are virtuous.

I have included elegant biscuits and everyday biscuits, as well as a recipe for dough that you can use to make cut-out biscuits. (Many doughs don't hold their shape well enough to be used for cut-outs, but this one does.) There are recipes that are great for when time is at a premium and you need a nutritious boost, perhaps to replace a missed breakfast or to take when travelling. Others are perfect for lunch boxes, or as healthy alternatives to grabbing a bar of chocolate.

Some of these biscuits do contain specialist ingredients, but they are easy to buy in most supermarkets and I am pretty sure they will not be lingering in your cupboards for long.

Super berry heroes

These are the superheroes of the biscuit world, but like the truest of heroes, they would not wish me to shout too loudly about their attributes.

MAKES ABOUT 20

115 g unsalted butter, softened

100 g golden granulated sugar

85 g soft dark brown sugar

1 tsp vanilla extract

1 egg

55 g spelt flour

75 g rye flour

1 tbsp gluten-free cocoa powder (e.g. Green & Black's)

½ tsp bicarbonate of soda

¼ tsp gluten-free baking powder

¼ tsp salt

¼ tsp freshly grated nutmeg

85 g rolled oats

75 g dried blueberries

50 g dried cranberries

YOU WILL ALSO NEED

Small ice-cream scoop (optional)

Preheat the oven to 170°C/Mark 3 and line two baking trays with non-stick baking paper.

Cream the butter, sugars and vanilla until very smooth. Scrape down the sides of the bowl, then add the egg and mix well.

Add all the dry ingredients, mixing until just combined, then use a large metal spoon to gently fold in the berries.

Using a small ice-cream scoop or two tablespoons, place dollops of the mixture on the prepared trays, spacing them at least 3 cm apart. Bake for 15–20 minutes, until dryish on top but still not quite firm. Set aside to firm up on their trays for at least 10 minutes, then use a palette knife to transfer them carefully to a wire rack to cool completely.

* Miranda's Variations

Add 50 g dark chocolate chips (70% cocoa solids) when folding in the berries.

Agave nectar and hazelnut boosters

Low-GI agave nectar replaces most of the sugar in this nutty booster. The wholesome hazelnuts and spelt flour put it top of the class and virtuously gluten-free.

MAKES AT LEAST 24

225 g hazelnuts, toasted
   and skinned (see
   page 7)
100 g unsalted butter,
   softened
50 g caster sugar
100 g agave nectar
1 egg
100 g spelt flour
¼ tsp salt
icing sugar, to dust

YOU WILL ALSO NEED
Small ice-cream scoop
   (optional)

Preheat the oven to 160°C/Mark 3 and line two baking trays with non-stick baking paper.

Place 200 g of the toasted hazelnuts in a food processor or blender and grind finely. Roughly chop the remaining 25 g and set aside.

Cream together the butter and sugar until very smooth. Pour in the agave nectar and beat well. Scrape down the sides of the bowl, then add the egg and mix well.

Gently fold in the flour, ground nuts and salt with a large metal spoon. Using a small ice-cream scoop or two tablespoons, place dollops of the dough on the prepared trays, spacing them at least 4 cm apart. Sprinkle generously with the chopped nuts, then flatten with a palette knife.

Bake for 20–25 minutes, until golden. Set aside to cool on their trays for 5 minutes, then use a palette knife to transfer them to a wire rack to cool completely. Dust with icing sugar before serving.

Fig rolls

These little rolls of goodness are crammed full of figs, orange zest and apples. They are far removed from the hard, dry fig rolls I used to think were a too-healthy alternative to a proper biscuit. Although delicious while still warm, they keep for up to a fortnight if stored in an airtight container.

MAKES AT LEAST 24

125 g unsalted butter, softened

75 g caster sugar

½ tsp vanilla extract

1 egg yolk

¼ tsp ground mixed spice

¼ tsp ground cinnamon

1 tbsp orange zest

150 g plain flour

50 g ground almonds

1 egg yolk plus 1 tbsp milk, to glaze

demerara sugar, for sprinkling

FOR THE FILLING

200 g dried figs, finely chopped

½ eating apple, cored and coarsely grated

1 tbsp grated orange zest

1 tbsp clear honey

2 tbsp freshly squeezed orange juice

Cream the butter, sugar and vanilla. Beat in the egg yolk, scraping down the sides of the bowl to ensure everything has combined. Add the spices, zest, flour and almonds and mix gently until incorporated. Bring the dough together with your hands and flatten into a disc. Wrap tightly in cling film and chill for about 30 minutes.

Meanwhile, put the fruit and zest for the filling into a bowl and chop even more finely using a pair of scissors or a sharp knife. Add the other filling ingredients, mix well and leave to steep until the dough has finished resting.

Preheat the oven to 170°C/Mark 3 and line two baking trays with non-stick baking paper.

Put the chilled dough between two sheets of cling film and roll into a rectangle about 3 mm thick. Slice the rectangle lengthways into three equal strips. Spoon a line of filling along the middle of each strip, brush one long edge with water and roll up. Turn the 'sausage' so that the seam is underneath and use a sharp knife to cut it into pieces about 3–4 cm long.

Using a palette knife, lift the pieces onto the prepared trays, spacing them at least 3 cm apart. Brush the top of each roll with the egg and milk glaze, then sprinkle with the demerara sugar. Bake for 20–25 minutes, or until golden brown. Set aside on their trays to cool a little, then use a palette knife to transfer them carefully to a wire rack to cool completely.

Omega cookies

These biscuits contain healthy omega fats in the form of nuts and seeds, and use apple sauce instead of butter. They are a great, healthy snack to have to hand, perfect for any time of the day when you feel the need for something to keep you going. They're fantastic too for journeys or outings, when you want something homemade that is also packed with goodness.

MAKES ABOUT 16

100 ml hemp seed oil or
    extra virgin olive oil
150 g soft light brown
    sugar
80 g clear honey
125 g apple sauce,
    homemade or from
    a jar
2 eggs, lightly beaten
1 tsp vanilla extract
160 g plain wholemeal
    flour
½ tsp bicarbonate of
    soda
½ tsp mixed spice
225 g rolled oats
30 g sunflower seeds
30 g pumpkin seeds
40 g linseed
50 g chopped walnuts
50 g sultanas

Preheat the oven to 180°C/Mark 4 and line two baking trays with non-stick baking paper.

Mix together the oil, sugar, honey and apple sauce. Add the eggs and vanilla and mix to combine. Fold in all the other ingredients and stir well to make a sticky dough.

Using your hands, roll the mixture into walnut-sized balls and place them on the prepared trays, spacing them at least 3 cm apart. (You can use two tablespoons to do this if you prefer.) Flatten the balls or dollops a little with the palm of your hand, then bake for 10–15 minutes, or until golden and just starting to caramelise around the edges. Leave to cool on their trays for at least 5 minutes, then use a palette knife to transfer them carefully to a wire rack to cool completely.

Orange spelt biscuits

Sweet, Mediterranean-inspired ingredients make up these biscuits, which are egg-, dairy- and gluten-free and show just what a delight alternative ingredients can be. The biscuits look pretty when cut into little flower shapes and glazed with a delicate orange icing.

MAKES AT LEAST 20

50 g rolled oats

250 g wholegrain spelt flour

1 tsp gluten-free baking powder

juice and grated zest of 1 orange

60 ml extra virgin olive oil

50 g caster sugar

2 tbsp clear honey or orange blossom honey

pinch of salt

FOR THE ICING

2 tbsp clear honey or orange blossom honey

150 g icing sugar

1 tbsp orange zest

1 tbsp orange juice

YOU WILL ALSO NEED

3 cm fluted or flower-shaped cutter

Whizz the oats in a food processor or blender until finely ground. Mix together with the spelt flour and baking powder.

In another bowl, mix together the orange juice and zest, olive oil, sugar, honey and salt. Add to the bowl of dry ingredients and mix well until a dough starts to form. Bring it together with your hands and flatten into two discs. Wrap each disc tightly in cling film and chill for about 30 minutes.

Preheat the oven to 180°C/Mark 4 and line two baking trays with non-stick baking paper.

Place each chilled disc of dough between two fresh sheets of cling film and roll out to a thickness of 3 cm. Using your chosen cutter, stamp out shapes and place on the prepared trays, spacing them at least 3 cm apart. Bake for about 12 minutes, until golden. Allow the biscuits to cool a little on their trays, then use a palette knife to transfer them carefully to a wire rack to cool completely.

Meanwhile, combine the icing ingredients, adding a little more water or orange juice if it is too stiff. When the biscuits are cold, spread roughly 1 teaspoon of the icing onto each biscuit and leave to set.

✳ Miranda's Variations

If you don't have time for grinding your own oats, use Ready Brek.

For coarser-textured biscuits, use the oats as they are, without grinding them.

Lemon and poppy seed polenta biscuits

Zingy, lemony and with the crunchy bite of polenta (cornmeal), these gluten-free biscuits taste 'sunny' and delicious. The lemon cream cheese filling complements them beautifully and is perfect for those looking for a butter-free icing.

MAKES ABOUT 15

175 g caster sugar

250 g quick-cook polenta

100 g rice or spelt flour

170 g unsalted butter, softened and cut into small chunks

zest of 2 lemons

2 eggs

½ tsp vanilla extract

20 g poppy seeds

icing sugar, to dust

FOR THE FILLING

200 g full-fat cream cheese

2 tsp lemon zest

1 tbsp icing sugar

2 tbsp caster sugar

2 tbsp lemon juice, or as required

YOU WILL ALSO NEED

Small ice-cream scoop (optional)

Put the sugar, polenta and flour into a large mixing bowl and whizz or mix well to combine. Add the butter and lemon zest and mix again until it looks like coarse breadcrumbs.

Put the eggs into a cup with the vanilla and beat lightly with a fork. Sprinkle the poppy seeds over the polenta mixture, then add the eggs and mix to make a sticky, wet dough.

Line a baking tray with non-stick baking paper, then use a small ice-cream scoop or two tablespoons to place walnut-sized balls of dough on it, spacing them at least 5 cm apart. Chill for at least 30 minutes.

Preheat the oven to 180°C/Mark 4. Bake the chilled biscuits for 10–12 minutes, or until pale golden and firm to the touch. Leave to firm up on their trays for at least 10 minutes, then use a palette knife to transfer them carefully to a wire rack to cool completely.

If you want to sandwich the biscuits together, put all the filling ingredients into a bowl and whizz with a hand mixer or beat with a wooden spoon until light and creamy. Add a little more lemon juice if the mixture seems too dry.

When the biscuits are completely cold, spread a layer of cream cheese filling onto the base of one biscuit and gently press a similar-sized biscuit on top. Dust with icing sugar before serving.

Gluten-free butter biscuits

The dough in this recipe is gluten-free, and can be used to make many different types of biscuit. It tastes similar to traditional shortbread, and can be sliced or cut into shapes, and used as a base for decorating.

MAKES ABOUT 24

100 g cornflour

160 g white rice flour

175 g unsalted butter, straight from the fridge, chopped into small pieces (or coarsely grated if making by hand)

50 g light muscovado sugar

50 g icing sugar

seeds from 1 vanilla pod or 1 tsp vanilla extract

¼ tsp salt

caster sugar, to sprinkle

YOU WILL ALSO NEED

4 cm round cutter

If you want to make the biscuits in a food processor, put all the ingredients in at the same time and whizz until a dough forms. If making the biscuits by hand, put both the flours into a bowl, rub in the grated butter with your fingers, then add the sugars, vanilla and salt and stir together with a wooden spoon. Use your hands to bring the dough together.

If you plan on rolling out the dough and cutting out shapes, flatten the dough into a disc and wrap tightly in cling film. If you want to make simple round biscuits, roll the dough into a log and wrap in cling film. Chill for about 30 minutes before rolling out, but the log can be chilled for up to 3 or 4 days if necessary.

Preheat the oven to 180°C/Mark 4 and line two baking trays with non-stick baking paper.

Place the chilled disc of dough between two sheets of cling film and roll out to a thickness of about 5 mm. Stamp out circles with a 4 cm cutter. If using a log of dough, cut slices about 5 mm thick. Use a palette knife to lift the circles onto the prepared trays, spacing them at least 3 cm apart. If time allows, chill for a further 15 minutes before baking.

Bake for 8–12 minutes, or until pale golden on top, a darker golden around the edges and mottled golden underneath. Sprinkle the biscuits with caster sugar as soon as they come out of the oven, then leave to firm up on their trays for at least 5 minutes. Use a palette knife to transfer them carefully to a wire rack to cool completely.

Crunchy peanut, raisin and chocolate chip biscuits

I have played around with lots of recipes for flourless peanut butter biscuits and, after a great deal of testing, I believe this to be the best. The double crunch of crunchy peanut butter and chopped unsalted peanuts tickles the taste buds and will please peanut fans no end. The addition of raisins and dark chocolate lifts the biscuits to a different level of enjoyment and satisfaction.

MAKES ABOUT 16

215 g crunchy peanut butter
125 g caster sugar
75 g soft dark brown sugar
25 g soft light brown sugar
1 egg, lightly beaten
½ tsp bicarbonate of soda
¼ tsp salt
75 g unsalted peanuts, roughly chopped
75 g raisins
75 g dark chocolate, 70% cocoa solids, coarsely chopped

Preheat the oven to 180°C/Mark 4 and line two baking trays with non-stick baking paper.

Put the peanut butter, sugars and egg into a bowl and mix with a wooden spoon to combine. Add all the other ingredients and mix again until the nuts, raisins and chocolate look evenly distributed.

Using your hands, roll the dough into lumpy, walnut-sized balls. Place them on the prepared trays, spacing them at least 4 cm apart, and flatten a little with the palm of your hand. Bake for 12–15 minutes, or until the biscuits look pale golden and fluffy. Set aside to cool on their trays.

Brazil nut bites

Flourless and packed with nourishing, unadulterated ingredients, these nutty, crunchy bites are so simple to make. Brazils are among the few nuts harvested from wild rainforest trees rather than grown on plantations, and in this recipe they are enhanced by the chewy texture of oats and the caramel taste of brown sugar. These are lovely biscuits to bake when you want to enjoy something that feels a little healthier. They are also delicious made with almonds.

MAKES ABOUT 15

55 g unsalted butter

70 g soft light brown sugar

1 egg

½ tsp vanilla extract

100 g Brazil nuts or almonds, roughly sliced

125 g rolled oats

Preheat the oven to 180°C/Mark 4 and line two baking trays with non-stick baking paper.

Melt the butter gently in a small pan and leave to cool a little. Add the sugar, egg and vanilla and whisk together until smooth. Fold in the nuts and oats.

Using a teaspoon, place dollops of the mixture on the prepared trays, spacing them at least 3 cm apart. Dip a large palette knife in water, then use it to flatten the biscuits as much as the nuts will allow – about 3 mm.

Bake for about 15 minutes, or until golden and fairly firm. Leave the biscuits to cool completely on their trays.

Healthy monkeys

Wholemeal flour, wheatgerm, banana and nuts create a medley of healthiness. These biscuits are ideal for days when you have missed breakfast or need a snack on the go. They're also fantastic for all cheeky monkeys to stash in their lunch boxes, or to gobble with a glass of milk when they get home from school (or work).

MAKES AT LEAST 24

200 g plain wholemeal
    flour
60 g wheatgerm
½ tsp bicarbonate of soda
½ tsp baking powder
¼ tsp sea salt
125 g unsalted butter,
    softened
145 g soft light brown
    sugar
2 large eggs
2 tsp vanilla extract
100 g dried banana chips,
    roughly chopped
75 g dark chocolate, 70%
    cocoa solids, chopped
    (optional)
75 g walnuts or toasted
    hazelnuts (see page 7)

YOU WILL ALSO NEED
Small ice-cream scoop
    (optional)

Preheat the oven to 190°C/Mark 5 and line two baking trays with non-stick baking paper.

Put the flour, wheatgerm, bicarbonate of soda, baking powder and salt into a large bowl, stir to combine and put to one side.

In a large mixing bowl, beat the butter until light and fluffy, then add the sugar and beat again until rich and creamy.

Add the eggs to the butter mixture a little at a time, scraping down the sides of the bowl to ensure each addition is completely mixed in before adding more. Add the vanilla and mix again.

Add half the flour mixture and fold in thoroughly using a large metal spoon. Add the remaining flour and stir again. Finally, add the banana chips, chocolate (if using) and nuts, stirring to distribute evenly.

Using a small ice-cream scoop or two tablespoons, place dollops of the dough on the prepared trays, spacing them at least 4 cm apart. Bake for 7–8 minutes, until barely golden. Leave to cool on their trays for about 5 minutes, then use a palette knife to transfer them carefully to a wire rack to cool completely.

Tip: Freeze two or three biscuits in a freezer bag, ready to put in a pocket or lunch box for a handy snack on the run. They will defrost on the way to school or work, and are a great alternative to a chocolate bar or processed snack.

Unbelievable chocolate biscuits

Rich and chocolatey but dairy- and gluten-free, these biscuits are 'unbelievably' delicious.

MAKES ABOUT 16

20 g walnuts, finely
    chopped
50 g pecans, finely
    chopped
70 g dark chocolate, 70%
    cocoa solids, finely
    chopped
35 g gluten-free cocoa
    powder (e.g. Green &
    Black's), sifted
215 g icing sugar, sifted
¼ tsp coarse sea salt
2 large egg whites

YOU WILL ALSO NEED
Small ice-cream scoop
    (optional)

Put the nuts and chocolate into a large bowl. Add the icing sugar, cocoa powder and salt, then stir to combine.

Whisk the egg whites until soft peaks form, then use a metal spoon or palette knife to fold them into the dry ingredients.

Preheat the oven to 170°C/Mark 3 and line two baking trays with non-stick baking paper.

Using a small ice-cream scoop or two tablespoons, place dollops of the mixture on the prepared trays, spacing them at least 4 cm apart. Bake for 15–20 minutes, or until dry and cracked on top. Set aside to firm up on their trays for about 4 minutes, then use a palette knife to transfer them carefully to a wire rack to cool completely.

Elegant pistachio puffs

Packed with pistachio nuts, these elegant puffs would look equally at home at a smart tea party, with coffee after dinner, or simply as a teatime treat. Made with egg whites, but with no need for butter, these are macaroon-like in their lightness.

MAKES AT LEAST 24

150 g shelled unsalted
    pistachios
25 g ground almonds
175 g caster sugar
4 tbsp finely grated
    orange zest
50 g plain flour
3 large egg whites
icing sugar, to dust

YOU WILL ALSO NEED
Small ice-cream scoop
    (optional)

Grind 125 g of the pistachios (see page 7) until only a few lumpy bits remain. Place them in a large bowl with the ground almonds, 115 g of the caster sugar and the orange zest. Sift in the flour, then stir with a wooden spoon to combine.

Preheat the oven to 180°C/Mark 4 and line two baking trays with non-stick baking paper.

Put the egg whites into a large bowl and whisk until soft peaks form. Add the remaining 60 g caster sugar a little at a time, whisking at a low speed after each addition. Keep whisking until the mixture is stiff and glossy.

Using a large metal spoon, add the egg mixture to the dry ingredients and gently fold together, using a figure of eight shape, until everything is well combined and smooth.

Using a small ice-cream scoop or two tablespoons, put dollops of the mixture on the prepared trays, spacing them at least 3 cm apart. Roughly chop the remaining 25 g pistachio nuts with a sharp knife and sprinkle a few on top of each dollop. Bake for about 15 minutes, until puffy and starting to turn golden brown.

Remove the biscuits from the oven and, using a sieve or shaker, immediately dredge with icing sugar. Leave them to cool on their trays for at least 20 minutes because they will stick and crumble if you try to move them too soon. Use a palette knife to transfer them carefully to a wire rack to cool completely. They keep well if stored in an airtight container.

7 CHILDREN'S PARTY BISCUITS

I adore children's parties; in fact I would go as far as to say that they are one of my greatest pleasures in life. I love the excitement and anticipation as we decide on a theme and talk about ideas for cakes and biscuits. I love to see the table laden with food and lots of happy-faced children choosing their favourites and chattering together.

The recipes in this chapter are aimed at making your life simple so that you can prepare lots of treats. The party rings, iced gems and chocolate fingers are all made from the same type of dough. The lollipop biscuits are very impressive but easy to master, and are great for party bags. The golden syrup biscuits topped with a swirl of chocolate and a Smartie look gorgeous and taste irresistible. More ambitious party-makers can delight their children and friends with dinosaur biscuits, ballerinas, rescue helicopters or other novel shapes (see page 158).

Above all, this chapter offers some simple ways to make parties extra special and create memories that you and your children will cherish. Many of these biscuits would make a nostalgic addition to adult tea parties as well.

Chocolate crunchers

These biscuits have a gorgeous crunchy base that tastes of golden syrup. Homely and delicious, they couldn't be easier to make, requiring no rolling out or cutting of shapes. I like to make them quite small and top with melted chocolate and a Smartie. Simple, scrummy and always gobbled up quickly.

MAKES AT LEAST 24

150 g unsalted butter, softened

40 g light muscovado sugar

40 g golden caster sugar

2 medium egg yolks

2 tsp golden syrup

1 tsp vanilla extract

250 g plain flour

¼ tsp bicarbonate of soda

½ tsp salt

FOR THE TOPPING

200 g milk chocolate

Smarties, little sweets, sugar sprinkles or icing decorations and flowers

Preheat the oven to 180°C/Mark 4 and line two baking trays with non-stick baking paper.

Cream the butter and sugars until light and fluffy. Scrape down the sides of the bowl, then add the egg yolks, golden syrup and vanilla and beat to combine. Sift the flour, bicarbonate of soda and salt into the mixture and stir until a dough starts to form. Bring the dough together with your hands to make a ball.

Tear off cherry-sized pieces of dough and roll into balls, 24 in total. Place them on the prepared baking trays, ensuring they are spaced at least 5 cm apart, and flatten a little with the palm of your hand. Bake for 15–20 minutes, or until golden. Remove from the oven and leave to cool on the trays until firm enough to lift onto a wire rack with a palette knife.

Break the chocolate into pieces and put into a heatproof bowl over a pan of simmering water. Watch the chocolate carefully and stir often until completely melted.

Place a sheet of baking paper underneath the rack on which the biscuits are cooling and use a teaspoon to smooth chocolate onto the top of each biscuit. Press a Smartie or some other decoration into the sticky chocolate and leave until cold and firm.

Party biscuits

The dough in this recipe is really easy and can be used to create three beautiful types of biscuit – party rings, iced gems and chocolate fingers – just what's needed when you're busy preparing for a birthday party.

Party rings are unanimously adored and my version, coloured with natural fruit, is particularly appealing. The central hole makes them ideal for placing onto fingers so they can be nibbled off, and my four-year-old daughter insists on having them for all her dolly tea parties. Use the tiny circles cut from the middle of the party rings to make a pretty batch of iced gems. The final portion of dough can be used to make chocolate fingers. In this case, they look edgy and retro, and always remind me of my own childhood parties.

MAKES ABOUT 20
PARTY RINGS AND 20
ICED GEMS AND 36
CHOCOLATE FINGERS

250 g unsalted butter, softened

100 g caster sugar

100 g soft brown sugar

2 eggs

450 g plain flour, sifted

¼ tsp baking powder

1 tsp vanilla extract

Cream the butter and sugars until light and fluffy. Beat in the eggs a little at a time, then add the flour and baking powder. Continue mixing until a dough starts to form.

Tip the dough onto a lightly floured surface and knead gently for about 20 seconds or until it comes together. Divide into three equal pieces and shape them into flat discs about 1–2 cm thick. Wrap each piece separately in cling film, then chill for at least 1 hour. (The dough could also be frozen at this point for future use.)

Line two baking trays with non-stick baking paper. Unwrap a disc of dough, place between two sheets of cling film and roll it out to a thickness of about 3 mm. Using the 5 cm cutter, stamp out 10 circles, then use the 1 cm cutter to make a hole in the middle of each one. Keep the middles, as these will be the bases for your iced gems. (If you are using a lid to cut the holes, you might need a cocktail stick to help remove the tiny rounds.) Repeat this process with another disc of dough so you end up with 20 rings and 20 gems.

FOR PARTY RINGS AND
ICED GEMS

2 x 500 g packets of royal
    icing sugar

2–3 tbsp blackcurrant
    fruit spread (I use St
    Dalfour sugar-free
    spreads), or natural
    food colouring

2–3 tbsp strawberry fruit
    spread, or natural food
    colouring

FOR CHOCOLATE
FINGERS

200 g milk chocolate

Multi-coloured sprinkles

YOU WILL ALSO NEED

3 cm round cutter

1 cm round cutter or
    metal lid from a vanilla
    extract bottle

Cocktail stick

Piping bag

No. 2 nozzle (optional)

Star or flower nozzle
    (optional)

Spacing them about 3 cm apart, put all the rings on one baking tray and all the gems on another – this is really important as the tiny ones will bake much faster than the larger ones and will need to come out of the oven sooner. Put the filled trays in the fridge for about 20 minutes.

Meanwhile, preheat the oven to 190°C/Mark 5 and prepare the finger biscuits. Place the remaining disc of dough between two sheets of cling film and roll into a skinny rectangle about 36 cm long, 7.5 cm wide and 1 cm thick. Straighten up the edges and cut into 36 strips about 1.5 cm wide. Place in the fridge to rest for about 20 minutes. (You can do this on the cling film until the baking trays are free again.)

Bake the gems for about 8 minutes and the rings for about 15 minutes, or until pale golden. Leave to cool on their trays for about 5 minutes, then use a palette knife to transfer them to a wire rack. Cool the empty trays as described on page 10 and line with fresh non-stick baking paper. Use a palette knife to lift the chilled fingers carefully onto the prepared trays, spacing them about 4 cm apart, then bake for about 10 minutes, or until pale golden and firm to touch. Leave to cool on their trays for about 5 minutes, then use a palette knife to transfer them to a wire rack to cool completely.

To decorate the rings and gems, make up the royal icing according to the packet instructions, then divide it between three bowls and cover with cling film.

Squash the blackcurrant spread through a sieve into one of the bowls of icing. Mix well with a palette knife until the icing is pale purple. It should be smooth and glossy but still hold its shape so that it doesn't run off the biscuit. Add more sieved blackcurrant spread if too thick, or more of the stiff royal icing if too runny. Cover with cling film, then make some pink icing using the strawberry spread in the same way.

Use a palette knife to smooth some icing on top of the ring biscuits, keeping it tidy around the hole and edges. Place on a sheet of baking paper while you do the next step.

Water down a little of the white royal icing and pop it into a piping bag fitted with a No. 2 nozzle. Alternatively, snip the corner off the bag to make a tiny hole about 2 mm wide. Now pipe lines across the still-wet iced biscuits. Gently pull the tip of a cocktail stick across the icing at a right angle to the lines you have iced to give a feathered effect. Leave to set for at least 5 hours, or ideally overnight, so that the icing goes completely hard.

To ice the gem-sized biscuits, place them on a sheet of baking paper and fill a piping bag fitted with a flower or star nozzle with stiff icing, white or coloured as desired. Alternatively, snip the corner off the bag to make a small hole about 3 mm wide. Pipe a swirl on top of each biscuit and scatter coloured sprinkles on some of them while the icing is still wet. Leave to harden at room temperature for a few hours to set completely.

Coating the finger biscuits is best done the evening before party day – any longer before and the chocolate might start turning cloudy. Melt the chocolate (see page 6), then set aside for about 20 minutes before using because this makes it easier to handle.

Once the biscuits are completely cold, place them on a sheet of baking paper. Drop one biscuit at a time into the melted chocolate, lift out with a fork and return to the baking paper to set. Repeat until all the biscuits are covered in chocolate. Scatter multi-coloured sprinkles on the ends of some of the biscuits. Put in the fridge or a cool place to set.

✳ Miranda's Variations

To make chocolate iced gems, make a thick chocolate ganache (see page 166), leave it to firm up, then fill a piping bag with it and ice the gem biscuits as before.

Cover a third of the finger biscuits with milk chocolate, a third with dark chocolate and the rest with white chocolate.

LOLLIPOP BISCUITS

Children love the novelty of lollipops, and what could be more novel than a biscuit on a stick? Shaped like flowers, stars, hearts or simple circles, they'll go down a treat. They're also ideal for birthday parties, especially if made in shapes to match the party theme. See the ideas below and let your imagination soar.

MAKES AT LEAST 12 LARGE BISCUITS

1 quantity vanilla or chocolate dough (see page 182 or 183)

150 g chocolate, or 500 g royal icing or roll-out sugarpaste icing, or 200 g boiled sweets, crushed

decorations, e.g. dolly mixtures, Smarties, icing flowers, chocolate buttons, sprinkles, etc.

YOU WILL ALSO NEED

Paper lollipop sticks (wooden skewers or wooden lolly sticks are good alternatives – make sure these are pressed very firmly into the biscuit dough or they might work loose)

Shaped cutters, at least 5 cm wide to accommodate stick

Cellophane bags

Ribbons

Flowerpot, jam jar or metal bucket plus sand or rice to place the finished lollipops in

Make the dough according to the recipe instructions and chill as specified. Place the chilled dough between two sheets of cling film and roll out to a thickness of 3 mm. Use a cutter to stamp out your chosen shapes (see ideas below).

Line two baking trays with non-stick baking paper and place rows of lolly sticks or skewers on them, spacing them about 5 cm apart? Place a dough shape carefully on top of each stick or skewer, ensuring that at least 3 cm of stick is hidden under each biscuit. Press down gently onto the stick, then put the filled trays in the fridge for about 20 minutes before baking in the preheated oven according to the dough recipe. Allow to cool on the trays for at least 15 minutes, then use a palette knife to transfer the biscuit lollipops to a wire rack and leave until completely cold.

Royal icing

Follow the instructions for decorating biscuits in Chapter 9 (see pages 184–188). Or simply use royal icing to pipe names, ages or patterns onto the biscuits. Alternatively, spread or drizzle royal icing over the biscuits and sprinkle with decorations while still wet. Set aside to harden.

Sugarpaste icing

Buy a packet of ready-coloured sugarpaste icing to fit with your theme. Lightly dust a work surface with icing sugar, then roll out the icing to a thickness of about 3 mm. Using the same cutter(s) you used to stamp out your biscuits, cut shapes out of the icing.

Make up 250 g of royal icing (see page 184), then use a palette knife to spread a thin layer of it over the biscuits. Carefully place a sugarpaste icing shape on top, pressing gently with your fingertips to ensure the shape is central and smoothly stuck down. Set aside to dry (for at least an hour) before decorating the top.

Chocolate

Melt some chocolate (see page 6). Allow to cool and stabilise a little, then spoon into a piping bag (see tip, page 184) and pipe patterns onto the biscuits. Alternatively, use a spoon to drizzle the chocolate over the biscuits, then stick some decorations on it. Leave to harden completely on a wire rack.

Astronauts & Pirates

THEME IDEAS

Flowers, Butterflies & Fairy Wands

Cut a selection of space- or pirate-themed shapes (e.g. rockets, ships) out of the dough, arrange them on lolly sticks or wooden skewers and bake as described opposite. Use the same cutters to cut shapes out of sugarpaste icing and stick them onto the biscuits with a little royal icing (as above). Decorate with stars, sprinkles or themed decorations, attaching them with a little royal icing.

Cut a selection of these shapes out of the dough, arrange them on lolly sticks (if making wands, use long wooden skewers or paper lollipop sticks) and bake as described above. Make up some royal icing (see page 184) and pipe patterns in pretty colours. Alternatively, put the icing into icing bottles and let the party girls decorate the biscuits themselves as part of the birthday party activities.

Tie a few pink or silver ribbons where the stick meets the biscuit to make a fairy wand.

Chocolate crispies

These biscuits are absolutely essential at every child's birthday party. And it is not just the children who adore them – the father of one of my children's friends insists on coming to all our parties, and once even took some chocolate crispies home with him – apparently it was his party bag.

MAKES ABOUT
24 BITE-SIZED
CRISPIES OR 12
LARGER ONES

110 g unsalted butter

110 g caster sugar

3 tbsp cocoa powder

1 tbsp syrup

1 tbsp milk

100 g cornflakes

YOU WILL ALSO NEED

Paper cases of the size
you wish to make

Put the butter, sugar, cocoa powder, syrup and milk in a large pan over a low heat and stir until completely melted. Do not let the mixture boil.

Using a wooden spoon, mix in the cornflakes a little at a time, making sure they are evenly coated before adding more.

Put your paper cases into 12-hole muffin tins and use a teaspoon to carefully fill each one with the mixture. Chill overnight. Remove from the fridge just before eating.

If there are any left over (highly unlikely), store them in a sealed container in the fridge. Great for midnight feasts.

8 PETIT FOURS

Dainty nibbles are irresistible, and this chapter celebrates the little biscuits called petit fours. These pretty morsels are great for nibbling with coffee, and a lovely way to end a meal, perhaps on a sharing plate so that people can pick and choose. Even when guests claim they can't manage another bite, they can't resist these.

Delicate biscuits, such as the macarons, fairy hats and dreamy orange delights, are perfect for a sophisticated tea party and look stunning on a cake stand. Others, such as millionaire's shortbread and lemon squares, can be made well in advance.

Most of the recipes in this chapter work well in large volumes and the quantities can easily be adapted for gatherings, such as weddings or christenings. They would also be lovely for buffets and parties where tempting goodies are required.

I hope you will have fun making these recipes. The best things come in small packages, and biscuits are no exception. Delectable and beautiful petit fours turn any event into a truly special occasion.

Orange dreamy delights

The lightest, dreamiest orange biscuits, these delightful mouthfuls are sandwiched with a layer of dark chocolate studded with bitter orange zest.

MAKES ABOUT 30
'SANDWICHES'

100 g unsalted butter, softened

300 g caster sugar

4½ tbsp freshly grated orange zest

100 ml sunflower oil or extra virgin olive oil

1 tsp freshly squeezed orange juice

250 g self-raising flour, preferably sifted

100 g dark chocolate, at least 70% cocoa solids

icing sugar, to dust

Cream together the butter, sugar and 3 tablespoons of the orange zest until the mixture is light and fluffy. Scrape down the sides of the bowl, then beat in the oil and orange juice until well combined. Add the flour and gently beat until a sticky dough forms.

Preheat the oven to 150°C/Mark 2 and line three baking trays with non-stick baking paper. If you have only two trays, bake the final batch of biscuits when the first two are done, but remember to cool the tray first (see page 10).

With floured hands, make cherry-sized balls of dough, ensuring they are smooth and fairly similar in size, and place them on the prepared trays, spacing them at least 3 cm apart. Bake for about 15 minutes, or until firm and pale golden. Watch them carefully as they colour quickly, and becoming too golden spoils the texture. Allow to cool on their trays for about 5 minutes, then use a palette knife to transfer them carefully to a wire rack. Leave until completely cold.

Melt the chocolate (see page 6), then stir in the remaining orange zest. Allow to cool for about 10 minutes.

Slide a sheet of baking paper underneath the wire rack. Put a teaspoonful of chocolate on the underside of each biscuit and gently press another biscuit on top. Put the filled biscuits on the rack and leave to set, ideally for a couple of hours. Dust with icing sugar and serve piled high on pretty cake-stands after dinner.

Intensely dark chocolate biscuits

Outrageously intense bites of dark chocolate gorgeousness –
I guarantee you'll love these biscuits, and they're really easy
to make.

MAKES AT LEAST 24

35 g unsalted butter

185 g dark chocolate, at
    least 70% cocoa solids

1 egg

25 g granulated sugar

50 g light muscovado
    sugar

¼ tsp vanilla extract

35 g plain flour

15 g cocoa powder

¼ tsp baking powder

¼ tsp salt

Preheat the oven to 170°C/Mark 3 and line two baking trays with non-stick baking paper.

Put the butter and 85 g of the chocolate in a heatproof bowl over a pan of simmering water. When it has melted, take it off the heat to cool a little.

Using a mixer, whisk together the egg, sugars and vanilla on a high speed for about 2 minutes. At a lower speed, gently mix in the melted chocolate until just combined. Now sift the flour, cocoa powder, baking powder and salt into the mixture and beat well.

Roughly chop the remaining 100 g chocolate into small chunks and fold about three-quarters of it into the biscuit mixture with a metal spoon.

Using a teaspoon, place tiny dollops of the mixture on the prepared trays, spacing them at least 3 cm apart. The best technique is to half-fill the teaspoon and push it off with another teaspoon. Tidy up the edges of the dollops with a small palette knife, then sprinkle the remaining chocolate pieces on top and press down a little with your fingers to flatten slightly.

Bake for about 10 minutes, until the surface of the biscuits looks dry but the chocolate pieces are still runny. Leave to cool on their trays for about 5 minutes, then place in the fridge for about 20 minutes to harden. This rapid cooling gives a delicious texture to the biscuits.

Milk chocolate pecan thins

A thick layer of the finest milk chocolate enrobes the slenderest sliver of pecan biscuit. You won't get much better than this.

MAKES ABOUT 24

65 g toasted pecan nuts
  (see page 7)

45 g rolled oats

20 g plain flour

¼ tsp salt

75 g unsalted butter

125 g soft dark brown
  sugar

1 tbsp golden syrup

1 tbsp treacle

1 tsp bicarbonate of soda

1 tsp vanilla extract

200 g milk chocolate, at
  least 54% cocoa solids

YOU WILL ALSO NEED

Pizza wheel (optional)

Preheat the oven to 170°C/Mark 3 and line three baking trays with non-stick baking paper. If you have only two trays, bake the final batch of biscuits when the first two are done, but remember to cool the tray first (see page 10).

Whizz the pecans in a food processor or crush with a rolling pin until finely ground. Add the oats and whizz again, then sift in the flour and salt and put to one side.

Bring the butter to the boil in a large, heavy pan, then add the sugar. Keep stirring over a medium heat until the sugar has completely dissolved and doesn't feel granular – about 2 minutes.

Reduce to a low heat and stir in the golden syrup and treacle. When these have completely melted, add the bicarbonate of soda and stir until frothy. Add the vanilla, then stir in the pecan mixture and remove from the heat.

Roll the mixture into cherry-sized balls and flatten as thinly as you can with a palette knife. Lift them onto the prepared trays, spacing them at least 4 cm apart. Bake for about 8 minutes, but check them after 7 minutes to be sure they aren't overbaking as they burn easily. It is hard to judge when they are ready as they are such a dark colour so if in doubt, take them out and let them cool: if they don't harden after about 10 minutes, put them back in the oven for another minute or so. Set aside to harden on their trays.

Melt the chocolate (see page 6), then cool for about 15 minutes.

When the biscuits are cold and hard, place them on a wire rack set over a sheet of baking paper. Spoon chocolate over the top of each biscuit and leave to set. If you are feeling indulgent, dip the whole biscuit in the chocolate. Use a fork or palette knife to transfer it to a fresh sheet of baking paper and leave to set.

Langues de chat with milk chocolate ganache

The name of these delicate sugar biscuits means 'cat tongues', which their shape was thought to resemble. Scrumptious alone, divine with pudding, and sublime when sandwiched with chocolate ganache, they are a chic addition to your repertoire.

MAKES ABOUT 16

100 g unsalted butter, softened

100 g caster sugar

2 egg whites

120 g plain flour, sifted

seeds from 1 vanilla pod

1 tsp vanilla extract

FOR THE GANACHE

150 ml double cream

1 tbsp caster sugar

tiny pinch of salt

50 g unsalted butter, softened

227 g milk chocolate, at least 37% cocoa solids (Green & Black's cooking chocolate is ideal)

50 ml milk

YOU WILL ALSO NEED

Disposable piping bag (optional)

Cream the butter and sugar with the vanilla seeds and extract. Add the egg whites a little at a time, mixing well after each addition. The mixture might look a little curdled; if so, scrape down the sides of the bowl, add 1 tablespoon of the flour and mix again. Now fold in all the flour with a metal spoon.

Preheat the oven to 200°C/Mark 6 and line two baking trays with non-stick baking paper.

Spoon the mixture into a piping bag or a freezer bag, then snip off the corner to make a hole about 1 cm wide. Pipe lines of the mixture onto the prepared trays, spacing them at least 4 cm apart. Bang the trays hard on the worktop to flatten out the biscuits, then bake for 12–15 minutes, or until pale golden all over.

Allow the biscuits to cool on their trays for at least 10 minutes before using a palette knife to transfer them carefully to a wire rack. They will feel spongy at first, but become crisper after about an hour.

Meanwhile, make the ganache. Place the cream, sugar and salt in a pan and bring to the boil. Remove from the heat immediately and add the butter and chocolate, stirring until completely melted. Allow to cool slightly, then stir in the cold milk until smooth and shiny. Set aside for about an hour to thicken.

When the ganache is thick and glossy, spread or pipe it onto the underside of half the biscuits, then put the plain halves on top.

Ratafia

Traditionally made with an extract of bitter almonds or peach kernels, ratafia are smaller, darker and chewier versions of macaroons. They feature in recipe books from as long ago as the eighteenth century and make pretty presents if wrapped in little cellophane bags. They are delicious with baked peaches and mascarpone.

MAKES ABOUT 24

25 g unsalted butter, softened

175 g caster sugar

1 tbsp plain flour

125 g ground almonds

2 egg whites

4 drops ratafia or almond extract

YOU WILL ALSO NEED

Rice paper (optional – though some of the biscuits might stick to the baking paper if you make them without rice paper)

Disposable piping bag (optional)

Preheat the oven to 170°C/Mark 3. Line two baking trays with non-stick baking paper and rice paper (if using).

Cream the butter and sugar. Add the flour and ground almonds and beat well to combine.

In a separate bowl, whisk the egg whites until stiff peaks form. Spoon the butter mixture onto the egg whites and fold in with a large metal spoon. Add the ratafia or almond extract and, beat to a smooth paste in a mixer or with a wooden spoon.

Spoon the mixture into a piping bag or a freezer bag, snip off the corner to give a hole about 1cm wide, and pipe small circles about 2 cm across onto the rice paper, spacing them at least 3 cm apart. Alternatively, use a teaspoon to put dollops of the mixture on the rice paper and tidy them with a palette knife. Bake for about 15 minutes, until they are golden and dry on top.

Set the biscuits aside to cool completely on their trays, then cut around them to leave just a small disc of rice paper on the bottom of each one or use a palette knife to lift them off the baking paper.

Heavenly lemon squares

Using the whole lemon in the mixture gives these squares
a very intense flavour. This is a great recipe for an occasion
when you have lots to bake as it's simple to put together and
elegant and can be made in advance.

MAKES 80

250 g unsalted butter,
    softened
90 g granulated sugar
1 tsp vanilla extract
250 g plain flour,
    preferably sifted
¼ tsp salt
icing sugar, to dust

FOR THE TOPPING
2 whole lemons,
    quartered and pips
    removed
200 g caster sugar
200 g granulated sugar
4 large eggs
25 g plain flour
50 g cornflour
¼ tsp salt
2 tbsp melted butter

Line a brownie tin with foil, leaving plenty overhanging the edges
so you can lift the contents out later.

Cream the butter and granulated sugar, then mix in the vanilla.
Add the flour and salt and mix gently until combined. The mixture
will be very sticky. Tip it into the prepared tin and press it in with
floured fingers. Prick all over with a fork and chill for 30 minutes, or
freeze for 10 minutes if you are in a rush.

Preheat the oven to 180°C/Mark 4 and bake the chilled mixture
for about 25 minutes, or until golden brown.

Meanwhile, make the topping. Put the lemons into a food
processor with the sugars. Whizz together until the lemons are
finely chopped – about 2 minutes should be long enough. Add
the eggs, flour, cornflour, salt and butter and whizz again until
completely smooth. Put into a large jug.

Remove the biscuit base from the oven and let it cool for 10
minutes. Reduce the oven temperature to about 170°C/Mark 3.
Put the cooled base back on the oven shelf and carefully pour the
lemon mixture over the top. Bake for another 30 minutes, or until
set – it should not wobble when you touch the middle. Set aside to
cool completely, ideally overnight in the fridge, before slicing.

Use the foil lining to lift the contents onto a chopping board,
then dredge with icing sugar. Use a large, sharp knife to cut into
tiny pieces about 2.5 cm square.

Banoffee biscuits

MAKES ABOUT 30

110 g unsalted butter,
    softened

70 g dark brown sugar

1 tsp vanilla extract

200 g plain flour, sifted

60 g cornflour

¼ tsp fine sea salt

60 g toasted walnuts
    (see page 7), coarsely
    chopped

2 tbsp demerara sugar

FOR THE TOPPING

50 g unsalted butter,
    softened

50 g soft light brown sugar

1 x 477 ml can condensed
    milk

large banana, cut into 20
    slices

juice of 1 lemon

1 tbsp demerara sugar

2 tbsp toasted walnuts
    (see page 7), finely
    chopped

icing sugar, to dust

YOU WILL ALSO NEED

Melon baller (optional)

Pastry brush

Cream the butter, sugar and vanilla in a mixer until light and fluffy. Add the flours, salt and half the walnuts and mix at a low speed until just combined. Now add about 40 ml cold water, a spoonful at a time, and mix in with a knife until the dough comes together; you might not need all the water.

Split the dough into four pieces, place each piece on a sheet of cling film and roll into a thin log about 2 cm in diameter. Wrap each log tightly in the cling film and chill for at least 1 hour. (If you don't need the full quantity of biscuits, I suggest you freeze half the dough at this point.)

Preheat the oven to 180°C/Mark 4 and line two baking trays with non-stick baking paper.

Combine the demerara sugar and remaining walnuts on a plate. Unwrap the dough and roll in the mixture until well coated. Using a bread knife, thinly slice each log into pieces 3 mm thick. Reshape a little into flat, round discs and place on the prepared trays, spacing them at least 3 cm apart. Sprinkle the tops with more of the sugar mixture and press in lightly with your fingers. Bake for about 15 minutes.

Meanwhile, prepare the topping. Put the butter, sugar and condensed milk in a pan and heat gently until the sugar has dissolved. Bring to the boil, stirring all the time, then turn down the heat and simmer gently for about 3 minutes, or until the mixture has thickened. Pour into a small bowl and leave to cool for about 30 minutes to reach a fudge-like consistency.

No longer than 1 hour before serving, cut the banana into thin slices and place on a sheet of greaseproof paper. Brush the slices with lemon juice to stop them from going brown.

Using a melon baller or a teaspoon, place a scoop of fudge topping on each biscuit and sit a slice of banana on top.

Combine the demerara sugar and walnuts in a bowl and sprinkle on top of the biscuits. Dust with icing sugar before serving.

Pistachio and white chocolate macarons

I made these on *The Great British Bake Off* and the judges loved them. I have had many requests for the recipe, so here it is.

MAKES ABOUT 20

75 g pistachios

125 g icing sugar

2 large egg whites, aged if possible (see box)

1 tbsp caster sugar

FOR THE FILLING

100 g white chocolate

100 g unsalted butter, softened

225 g icing sugar, sifted

50 g pistachios, ground

YOU WILL ALSO NEED

Empty cereal packet or sheet of thin card

2 pence piece

Pencil

Preheat the oven to 190°C/Mark 5 and line two large baking trays with non-stick baking paper.

Whizz the pistachios and icing sugar in a food processor until you have a fine powder, then sift to remove any lumps.

Put the egg whites into a bowl and whisk to soft peaks. Add the caster sugar and whisk again, until glossy. Fold into the pistachio mixture, then put into a piping bag and snip off the corner to make a hole about 1 cm wide.

Take a piece of card roughly the same size as your baking tray (an empty cereal packet is ideal) and draw 20 times around a 2 pence piece, spacing the circles 3 cm apart. Slide the card under the baking paper on one of the baking trays, then use it as a template to pipe 20 blobs. Carefully slide it out when you have finished and repeat this process on the second baking tray. Allow the piped macarons to stand for about 15 minutes (or 1 hour on a rainy day) so they dry out a little and a skin starts to form. During this time, keep them away from the oven and anything steamy. Swap the trays over and bake for another 4 minutes, or until dry on top, then set aside to cool.

To make the filling, melt the chocolate (see page 6), then set aside to cool for about 15 minutes.

Cream the butter and icing sugar until very light. Using a metal spoon, fold in the melted chocolate and pistachio nuts.

Pair up matching sizes of macaron before you start to fill them. Put a small blob of buttercream on the underside of one half, gently press the other half on top and twist a little to fill evenly. The macarons can be eaten straight away, but are even better if left overnight.

Brown sugar and fig macarons

Chic and sophisticated are the words that best describe these macarons – a delectable combination of the lightest brown sugar meringue with a filling of caramelised fresh figs.

MAKES ABOUT 25

35 g toasted almonds
(see page 7)

¼ tsp ground cinnamon

1 tsp plain flour

100 g icing sugar

40 g ground almonds

2 egg whites, aged if
possible

45 g granulated sugar

20 g dark brown sugar

FOR THE FILLING

4 large fresh figs, roughly
chopped

1 tbsp balsamic vinegar

Preheat the oven to 180°C/Mark 4 and line two baking trays with non-stick baking paper.

Put the toasted almonds, cinnamon and flour in a food processor and whizz until finely ground. Add the icing sugar and ground almonds and whizz again until very fine. Sift the mixture into a large mixing bowl and reserve the contents of the sieve (the coarse pieces of nut are returned at the end to give a delicious toasted flavour, but it is still essential to sift at this stage as it gives a finer, airier texture).

In a separate bowl, whisk the egg whites until they form soft peaks and are very glossy. Sift in both the sugars, then whisk again for another 2 minutes, until the egg whites are stiff, firm and shiny.

Using a large metal spoon, scrape all the egg whites onto the dry ingredients and fold in gently until well combined. Fill a piping bag with the mixture and cut off the corner to leave a hole 1 cm wide.

Take a piece of card roughly the same size as your baking tray (an empty cereal packet is ideal) and draw 25 times around a 2 pence piece, spacing the circles 3 cm apart. Slide the card under the baking paper on one of the baking trays, then use it as a template to pipe 25 circles of the mixture. Carefully slide it out when you have finished and repeat this process on the second baking tray.

YOU WILL ALSO NEED
Disposable piping bag
Empty cereal packet or
sheet of thin card

Allow the piped macarons to stand for about 15 minutes (or 1 hour on a rainy day) so they dry out a little and a skin starts to form. During this time, keep them away from the oven and anything steamy.

Bake on the middle and bottom shelves of the oven for about 7 minutes, then swap the trays and turn them around. Check again after another 5 minutes, and remove after a final 3 minutes, unless they still appear sticky when you try to move one. Set aside to cool completely on the trays. The macarons are now ready to fill, or can be frozen in pairs until you need them.

To make the filling, spread the figs out on a large baking tray, sprinkle with the vinegar and bake at 125°C/Mark ½ for about 1 hour. Switch off the oven and leave the figs inside until they have gone completely cold. Remove and blend to a smooth paste, then keep in a sealed jar in the fridge until you are ready to use it.

Pair up matching sizes of macaron before you start to fill them. Put a small blob of balsamic fig paste on the underside of one half, gently press the other half on top and twist a little to fill evenly. The macarons can be eaten straight away, but are even better if left overnight.

Tip: As soon as you start thinking you might want to make macarons, separate two eggs. Cover the whites with foil and leave in a cool place (not the fridge) for up to 48 hours. It is worth doing this even if you leave them for only a couple of hours – the longer the whites rest, the better they will whisk up. If covered and stored in the fridge, the whites will keep for up to seven days, but must be brought back to room temperature before using. Cover the yolks with cling film and pop them in the fridge.

Fairy meringue hats

Stunning, unusual and bound to win you compliments, these enchanting little biscuits are topped with tiny meringues.

MAKES ABOUT 40

1 quantity chocolate,
    vanilla or lemon
    biscuit dough (see
    pages 182–183)

MERINGUE TOPPING

2 large egg whites

½ tsp cream of tartar

100 g caster sugar

YOU WILL ALSO NEED

1 cm round cutter or
    metal lid from a vanilla
    extract bottle

Cocktail sticks

Piping bag or disposable
    piping bag

Star or flower nozzle
    (optional)

Make the dough, then wrap tightly in cling film and chill for at least 1 hour.

Line two baking trays with non-stick baking paper. Put the chilled dough between two fresh sheets of cling film and roll out to a thickness of 2–3 mm. Using a 1 cm cutter or metal bottle lid, stamp out circles. (If using a lid, you might need a cocktail stick to help remove the tiny rounds.) Place them on the prepared baking tray and chill for about 10 minutes, or until needed.

Preheat the oven to 180°C/Mark 4 and bake the biscuits for about 8 minutes. Set aside on the tray to cool completely. Reduce the oven temperature to 140°C/Mark 1.

In a mixer, whisk the egg whites and cream of tartar until stiff, then add half the sugar and whisk on a lower speed until incorporated. Add the remaining sugar and whisk until stiff and glossy. Spoon into a piping bag fitted with a star or flower nozzle, or snip off the corner of a disposable piping bag to make a hole about 1 cm wide.

Pipe meringue onto the top of each biscuit, then return them to the oven and bake for a further 20 minutes at the lower temperature. After this time, switch the oven off, without opening the door, and leave the biscuits to cool inside for 1 hour. Alternatively, turn the oven down to its lowest temperature and leave the biscuits inside for about another 15 minutes. They should be slightly golden around the edges, but mainly white.

Millionaire's shortbread

A much-loved favourite at teatime and a wonderful after-dinner treat, this crunchy shortbread has a thick layer of fudge topped with chocolate. The biscuits keep well, so can be made a few days before they are needed and kept in the fridge. They look pretty cut into small squares and put in petit-four cases as part of a tea-party menu.

MAKES AT LEAST 60
SMALL PIECES

225 g plain flour
75 g caster sugar
150 g butter, at room
    temperature, chopped

FOR THE FUDGE
100 g unsalted butter
100 g soft light brown
    sugar
2 x 477 ml cans
    condensed milk

FOR THE TOPPING
255 g dark chocolate, at
    least 70% cocoa solids
½ tsp sunflower oil
    (optional)

Preheat the oven to 180°C/Mark 4. Line a brownie tin with foil and baking paper, leaving plenty overhanging the edges to help you to lift the shortbread out later.

Stir together the flour and sugar, then rub in the butter with your fingertips. When it resembles fine breadcrumbs, pour the mixture into the prepared tin. Squash down gently to make a firm base, then bake for about 20 minutes, or until starting to turn golden. Set aside to cool in the tin.

To make the fudge, put the butter, sugar and condensed milk in a pan and heat gently until the sugar has dissolved. Bring to the boil, stirring all the time, then simmer very gently for about 3–4 minutes, or until thick.

Pour the fudge over the cooled shortbread base and spread evenly. Chill for about 1 hour to set.

Once the fudge has set, melt the chocolate (see page 6), stir in the oil (if using) and spread it carefully over the top of the fudge. Return to the fridge to set.

Lift the finished shortbread out of the tin and transfer to a cutting board. Cut into 2.5 cm squares using a large, sharp knife and put each square into a mini paper case to match the theme of your tea party.

Salted caramel sandwiches

Crunchy biscuits flavoured with salty caramel and almonds are delicious on their own, but even better if sandwiched with salted dark chocolate ganache. If you want, the ganache can be made in advance and stored in the fridge, but allow it to come up to room temperature for an hour before you sandwich the biscuits.

MAKES ABOUT 30

50 g unsalted butter

50 g caster sugar

35 g soft light brown sugar

2 tbsp double cream

55 g unskinned almonds, chopped

40 g plain flour, preferably sifted

½ tsp sea salt

FOR THE GANACHE

125 g dark chocolate, at least 70% cocoa solids

25 g dark chocolate, about 40% cocoa solids, such as Bourneville

150 ml double cream

150 g light muscovado sugar

2 tsp sea salt flakes

YOU WILL ALSO NEED

Piping bag (optional)

Preheat the oven to 180°C/Mark 4 and line three baking trays with non-stick baking paper. If you have only two trays, bake the final batch of biscuits when the first two are done, but remember to cool the tray first (see page 10).

Put the butter, sugars and cream in a pan and heat gently to melt together. Bring to the boil and boil for 1 minute, stirring all the time. Add the almonds, flour and salt and stir well to combine.

Working quickly, as the mixture is hard to handle when it sets, place half teaspoonfuls of it on each of the prepared trays, spacing them at least 3 cm apart. (I use a metric half-teaspoon levelled off, then scoop the mixture out with a small palette knife.) Flatten the spoonfuls a little, then bake for 8–10 minutes, until golden and flat. Allow to cool on their trays for 10 minutes, then use a palette knife to transfer them carefully to a wire rack. Leave until cold.

To make the filling, finely chop both types of chocolate and put into a heatproof bowl with all the other ingredients. Place the bowl over a pan of simmering water and keep stirring until everything has melted and is shiny and thick. Remove from the heat and allow to stand (not in the fridge) for about 1 hour to thicken further.

Spoon or pipe the filling onto the underside of half the biscuits, top with the remaining biscuits and press together gently.

Prune and almond cantucci

MAKES ABOUT 30

175 g ready-to-use
     pitted prunes
4 tbsp brandy
2 eggs
250 g caster sugar
½ tsp vanilla extract
seeds from 1 vanilla
     pod
225 g plain flour
1 tsp bicarbonate of
     soda
¼ tsp salt
50 g unskinned
     almonds, roughly
     chopped
25 g ground almonds
1 egg yolk beaten with
     2 tbsp milk, to glaze
2 tbsp caster sugar, for
     sprinkling

Soak the prunes in the brandy, ideally overnight.

Preheat the oven to 150°C/Mark 2 and line three baking trays with non-stick baking paper. If you have only two trays, bake the final batch of biscuits when the first two are done, but remember to cool the tray first (see page 10).

Put the eggs, sugar, vanilla and seeds into a large mixing bowl and whisk together on the highest speed for about 4 minutes, until you have a voluminous, pale and mousse-like mixture.

Sift the flour, bicarbonate of soda and salt into the mixture, then fold in using a large metal spoon.

Drain the prunes, reserving the brandy, and roughly chop them. Add them to the flour mixture along with the chopped and ground almonds and 1½ tablespoons of the reserved brandy and fold in gently. Leave the mixture to stand for about 10 minutes.

Lightly flour a work surface and spoon about a third of the dough onto it. With floured hands, roll it into a rough log shape – don't worry if it seems messy and sticky – then carefully lift it onto one of the prepared trays. Repeat to make two more logs.

Brush the egg mixture over each of the logs – you won't need all of it – then sprinkle generously with caster sugar. Bake for 35–40 minutes, swapping the trays around roughly every 12 minutes to bake evenly.

Take them out of the oven and reduce the temperature to 140°C/ Mark 1. Cool the logs for about 10 minutes, then use a large, sharp knife to cut them into slices 1–2 cm wide. Using a palette knife, carefully arrange the slices flat-side down on the baking trays.

Once the oven has reached the lower temperature, return the trays to it and bake for 15 minutes. Use a palette knife to turn the slices over. Bake for another 15–20 minutes, then cool and harden for at least 1 hour before serving.

These biscuits can be made in advance and will keep for a couple of months if stored in an airtight container between layers of baking paper.

Tiny sticky toffee puddings

These fun little biscuits are bound to cause great delight when they appear. What could be more scrumptious than a tiny biscuit portion of sticky toffee pudding? Serve just as they are with coffee, or add a blob of clotted cream or vanilla ice cream for a more substantial pudding. Added to a cake-stand, they make a beautiful addition to a tea party.

MAKES ABOUT 20

85 g pitted dates, chopped

¼ tsp bicarbonate of soda

100 g unsalted butter, softened

125 g golden granulated sugar

75 g dark brown sugar

1 tsp vanilla extract

1 egg, lightly beaten

250 g plain flour

1/2 tsp baking powder

¼ tsp salt

75 g vanilla fudge, finely chopped (fingers of fudge will do)

FOR THE TOPPING

75 g soft light brown sugar

60 ml condensed milk

2 tbsp unsalted butter

Put the dates in a small pan with 2 tablespoons of water and bring to the boil. Remove from the heat and add the bicarbonate of soda. Stir and set aside to cool.

Cream the butter, sugars and vanilla. Add the egg and beat well to combine. Sift in the flour, baking powder and salt and mix gently on a low speed or by hand. Fold in the dates and fudge to make quite a sticky dough. Keep the unwashed date pan for making the sticky drizzle.

Preheat the oven to 180°C/Mark 4 and line two baking trays with non-stick baking paper.

Using a small ice-cream scoop or two tablespoons or floured hands, make cherry-sized balls of dough and place them on the prepared trays, spacing them at least 2 cm apart. Flatten them a little with your hand and bake for about 15 minutes. Set aside to cool on their trays.

To prepare the sticky toffee topping, put the sugar and condensed milk in the unwashed date pan and stir over a medium heat until the sugar dissolves – you should not be able to feel the grains when you pull the wooden spoon across the bottom of the pan. Remove from the heat and beat in the butter until smooth and glossy.

When the biscuits are cool, spoon the sticky toffee topping over each one. They are delicious while still warm, but you can leave them to set if you'd prefer a firmer topping.

9 MAKING & DECORATING CELEBRATION BISCUITS

Biscuits are perfect for celebrating all the important events in life. They are personal and packed with love; they show your friends and family just how much you care for them; and they allow you to add personal touches and details that no one else can. Even the shapes, your style of handwriting in the icing and choice of decorations will make those who receive your biscuits know at a glance just how important they are to have been given such a special present. These biscuits say you care.

It is important that beautifully decorated biscuits not only look divine but also taste delicious. So many recipes or biscuits you can buy for special occasions are hard and dry as they are overbaked to provide a sturdy base for icing or to give them a longer shelf life. The recipes in this chapter are different: although they might look too beautiful to eat, they will be devoured and remembered for their wonderful flavour and perfect bake.

All these biscuits need time and a bit of patience to put together, but they can be made in stages if you need to do other things. Planning and preparation will produce the best results. Work backwards from the event you are preparing for and ensure you have plenty of time for the dough to rest, the biscuits to cool, the icing to set, the decorations to be applied and, of course, for the final wrapping or presentation.

Choosing the right biscuit dough

There are three recipes for biscuit bases in this chapter (as well as a means of varying one of them). They are all suitable for decorating with royal icing, but they can also be dipped in chocolate, sandwiched with ganache or buttercream, or enjoyed unadorned. The choice is yours.

Uncooked biscuit dough will keep well for a few days in the fridge provided it is tightly wrapped in cling film. Once baked, biscuits need to be stored in an airtight container until you are ready to ice them.

Those made from the gingerbread dough will keep the longest and can be made up to three weeks before the biscuits are iced. After decoration, they will also keep well in little cellophane bags for up to six weeks.

Those made from the vanilla or chocolate dough stay firm and keep well, but will need to be eaten after about a week if they are to be enjoyed at their best. If you are making the citrus zest variation of the vanilla dough, the biscuits will keep for less than a week. However, I am sure whichever you choose, they won't be around long enough for you to worry about their keeping time.

Resting dough

It is important to follow the recipe instructions for resting your dough. All those made in this chapter need to have a double rest in the fridge – once after making, and again after cutting out. This is really important to stop your biscuits spreading or losing their shape while in the oven. There are more useful tips about making and baking biscuits in the introduction (see pages 8–11).

Choosing shapes

When choosing what shape to make your biscuits, consider what will work together as a collection. For a new baby, for example, you might want bootees, bibs, vests, ducklings and suchlike.

Having chosen your shape(s), it is often useful to make some in a slightly larger size to allow for writing longer messages. Think about what you want to put on the biscuits before you choose your cutters, as there is nothing more frustrating than trying to squeeze a message onto too small a biscuit.

If you prefer not to make fancy shapes, simple square or round biscuits (cut with a pizza wheel, sharp knife or round metal cutter) can also look beautiful when decorated.

Whatever shape you choose, they all work well with the dough recipes that follow and hold their shape beautifully.

Biscuit Doughs

Vanilla pod butter biscuits

These biscuits taste delicious yet remain firm making them ideal for icing and decorating. They will last well in an airtight container or tightly sealed cellophane bag, iced or un-iced, and will still taste fresh a week after making. For a citrussy biscuit, you could swap the vanila seeds for lemon or orange zest, but be aware that they will soften more quickly.

MAKES ABOUT 24
200 g unsalted butter, softened
200 g caster sugar
seeds from 2 vanilla pods or finely grated
    zest of 1 lemon or 1 orange
1 large egg, lightly beaten
400 g plain flour, preferably superfine 00

YOU WILL ALSO NEED
6 cm cutters (to make 24 biscuits)

Cream the butter, sugar and vanilla seeds or zest in a mixer until light and fluffy. Beat in the egg, then add the flour and mix on a low speed until a dough forms. If not using a mixer, bring the dough together with your hands. Shape into two flat discs, wrap tightly in cling film and chill for at least 30 minutes.

Preheat the oven to 180°C/Mark 4 and line two baking trays with non-stick baking paper.

Roll out each disc of chilled dough between two sheets of cling film, and cut into your chosen shapes. Place them on the prepared trays, spacing them about 3 cm apart, and chill for at least 15 minutes.

Bake for about 9 minutes, until golden brown at the edges. Allow to cool on the trays for about 5 minutes, then use a palette knife to transfer them carefully to a wire rack. Leave until cold before decorating.

Gorgeous gingerbread

This traditional gingerbread, with its almost caramel flavour, is a lovely dough for making Christmas tree decorations or gingerbread houses.

MAKES ABOUT 30
175 g soft brown sugar
4 tbsp clear honey
1 tbsp treacle
1 tbsp golden syrup
1 tbsp freshly squeezed orange juice
2 tbsp ground ginger
½ tbsp ground cinnamon
1 tsp vanilla extract
200 g unsalted butter, roughly chopped
450 g plain flour
1 tsp bicarbonate of soda
¼ tsp salt

YOU WILL ALSO NEED
6 cm cutters (to make 30 biscuits)

Put the sugar, honey, treacle, syrup, orange juice, spices and vanilla into a pan and bring to the boil, stirring regularly. Take the pan off the heat and add the butter, stirring until the butter has melted and the mixture is glossy. Pour into a mixing bowl and cool for 1 hour.

Sift the flour, bicarbonate of soda and salt onto the cold sugar mixture and mix to form a dough. Divide the dough into three pieces, roll each one into a ball and flatten into a disc. Wrap tightly in cling film and chill for 1 hour. If you're making the dough in advance, it will keep well in the fridge for up to a week, but it will go very hard, so you will need to leave it at room temperature for 1 hour before rolling it out.

Preheat the oven to 180°C/Mark 4 and line two baking trays with non-stick baking paper.

Roll out each disc of chilled dough between two sheets of cling film, then stamp out your shapes. Place on the prepared trays, spacing them at least 3 cm apart, and chill for another 15 minutes. Bake for about 12 minutes, or until golden. Allow to cool on the trays for 10 minutes, then use a palette knife to transfer the biscuits to a wire rack. When completely cold, decorate as you wish.

The undecorated biscuits will keep for a few months if stored in an airtight container.

Irresistible chocolate biscuits

These make a stunning base for icing or for decorating with melted chocolate.

MAKES 24
55 g dark chocolate (Bourneville or Belgian is best)

200 g unsalted butter, softened
160 g caster sugar or vanilla sugar
50 g golden syrup
1 egg, lightly beaten
350 g plain flour
50 g cocoa powder

YOU WILL ALSO NEED
5–6 cm cutters (to make 24 biscuits)

Melt the chocolate (see page 6). Cream the butter with the sugar, then beat in the melted chocolate and syrup until light and fluffy.

Add the egg and mix until well combined. Sift in the flour and cocoa powder, then mix until a dough starts to form. Bring it together with your hands and divide in half. Roll each piece into a ball and flatten into a disc (don't worry if they are a bit sticky). Wrap each disc tightly in cling film and chill for at least 1 hour.

Line two baking trays with non-stick baking paper.

Roll out each disc of chilled dough between two sheets of cling film, then stamp out your shapes. Place on the prepared trays, spacing them at least 3 cm apart, and chill for another 15 minutes.

Preheat the oven to 180°C/Mark 4 and bake the shapes for about 10 minutes, until the surface is dry and the base is firm. Allow to cool on the trays for 10 minutes, then use a palette knife to transfer the biscuits to a wire rack. When completely cold, decorate as you wish.

Icing & Decorating

The pages that follow give you all the recipes you require for making different types of icing. They also include ideas for colouring and flavouring it.

ROYAL ICING

Royal icing is traditionally made with egg white and sets hard. To avoid using raw egg, you can use pasteurised dried egg white instead or buy ready-mixed royal icing sugar to which you just add water.

Royal icing made with dried egg white can be made a few days in advance and will keep well in an airtight container in a cool place. If made with raw egg whites, it should be used the same day.

MAKES ENOUGH TO COVER AT
LEAST 24 BISCUITS

13 g Merriwhite (dried pasteurised egg white powder)

500 g icing sugar

150 ml warm water

1 tbsp lemon juice or flavouring, such as lemon, orange or lime juice, rosewater, orange blossom water (optional)

Put the dry ingredients into a bowl, add the warm water and lemon juice and beat well to form a thick paste (this will take about 7 minutes in a mixer on the highest speed). You can then add a tiny bit of extra water to make it a good thickness for piping, and even more water to make run-out icing. To check the consistency of run-out icing, pull a spoon through the mixture – the icing should return to being completely smooth.

ICING TIPS

- Make sure your biscuits are completely cold before you start to ice them.
- Cocktail sticks are extremely useful for encouraging icing into difficult corners and for arranging decorations.
- Colour pastes are essential for colouring icing, so it is worth buying a few of your favourites. Just a spot is needed because they are intense.
- It gives a tidier finish to choose a maximum of three colours for your collection of biscuits. Try to stick to a colour theme and everything will look more organised and thought through. I like to include white as one of the colours to give a fresh look and to tie the decorations together.
- Collect little plastic pots with lids to store different colours and consistencies of icing until you need them.
- Mix up more icing than you think you need. It is very frustrating to run out and have to mix up more just when you thought you had almost finished decorating.
- To fill a piping bag easily, stretch it over the top of a jug – this will keep it wide open and make it much easier to spoon in the icing.
- Non-stick plastic icing bags with a nozzle attachment allow you to change the nozzle

without emptying the bag. They will save you time and lots of mess and frustration.

- Keep your icing nozzle tightly wrapped in cling film or in a clean, damp kitchen cloth to make sure it doesn't dry out when you are not using it.
- Pipe an outline of your design in royal icing and make sure it is completely firm before flooding it with runny icing.
- Icing bottles are really useful for runny icing, and speed up the flooding process enormously. In this case, they are much tidier and quicker to use than a piping bag.

Step-by-step guide to icing and flooding

1. Make a batch of royal icing and divide it between four separate bowls. I usually leave two bowls white (one for stiff icing and one for watering down), and colour the other two bowls. Three colours gives a simple and effective colour scheme, but if you want to use more colours, you will need to divide the icing between more bowls. Make sure the bowls are covered tightly with cling film when you are not working with the icing, otherwise the contents will dry out.

2. To colour the icing, use a cocktail stick to dab tiny spots of colouring paste onto it and mix well with a palette knife to get a perfectly even colour. Remember, the paste is very strong, so build up the icing to the shade you want in tiny amounts. If you overdo it, mix in some more white icing to soften the tone.

3. Fill a piping bag with about 6 cm of stiff, white royal icing (add a few drops of water if it seems too stiff to pipe with). Using a No. 2 icing nozzle, pipe an outline onto the biscuit 2–3 mm from the edge, making sure there are no gaps for the runny icing to escape from later. The idea is to create a little icing frame around each biscuit. If you want parts of the biscuits to be flooded in different colours, you need to pipe further lines of royal icing to define these sections. Once you have completed the outlines on all the biscuits, set them aside to harden.

4. When the outline icing is completely firm, take one colour of icing and loosen slightly by adding a few drops of water just a tiny amount at a time and mixing well. To test if you have the right consistency, pull a palette knife through the middle of the icing, then lift it out – the icing should return to normal and there should be no mark left by the knife. Repeat for all the colours you are using.

5. Fill icing bottles or piping bags fitted with a wide-ended nozzle with the runnier icing. Alternatively, fill freezer bags with the icing and snip off the corner to leave a hole no larger than 3 mm. Gently squirt the icing onto the biscuit to fill or flood inside the outline you have already piped. Use a

cocktail stick to spread out the icing and to encourage it into any awkward corners. Repeat to fill each part of the biscuits with your chosen colour(s).

6. The icing will need to harden for 3–4 hours before you can decorate on top of it. Be patient as it can look set, but will crack when you attempt to decorate if it has not dried for long enough.

7. For extra shiny icing, leave the biscuits to harden under a bright light – a desk lamp is perfect.

8. Once the flooding has completely set, use stiff royal icing to decorate the iced biscuits with dots or patterns, or personalise them with names, dates, etc. I use white icing, but you can use coloured if you prefer. Set aside to harden.

9. Use sugar florist paste to make flowers, stars or pretty decorations, or buy ready-made icing decorations. Attach these to the biscuits with a tiny dab of royal icing. Set aside to harden.

10. Once the decoration has completely hardened, pack, wrap or arrange your beautiful biscuits as you wish.

Shortcut icing method

Using roll-out icing is the speedy way to make decorated biscuits, especially if you are making lots of them for a wedding or big party. However, please bear in mind that the finished result will not taste as wonderful as the royal iced biscuits above.

Choose ready-to-roll white or coloured icing to suit your theme. Lightly dust a work surface with icing sugar, then roll out the icing to a thickness of about 3 mm. Using the same cutter used to make your biscuits, stamp out shapes. Spread a thin layer of royal icing on top of each biscuit, then gently press the icing cut-out on top. Leave to dry completely before decorating the top with royal icing or decorations as in steps 8 and 9 above.

Decorating with chocolate

Melt about 200 g white or dark chocolate (see page 6). Allow to cool a little and stabilise before putting it in a piping bag fitted with a No. 2 nozzle and piping it onto the biscuits. Alternatively, dip half of each biscuit into the melted chocolate. In both cases, leave to one side until completely set.

Popular themes

There are certain life events – such as birthdays, weddings and new babies – that are so special they demand to be marked with something out of the ordinary. I can think of no better way than making a collection of biscuits tailored to each occasion, and some of my favourite ideas are given opposite.

WEDDING COLLECTION

Make one of the biscuit doughs on pages 182–183, then cut into shapes such as wedding cakes, dresses, shoes, hearts, churches or a special theme from the wedding. Once iced, with perhaps a few simple decorations to make them look extra pretty, these biscuits make a stunning gift for the happy couple, or can be given to the wedding guests as 'favours'. I often wrap them in little cellophane bags tied with ribbon so they can be taken home, but they look equally lovely placed on white linen tablecloths beside each place setting. You can even add a personal touch by icing the guests' names onto plain biscuits to use as place cards.

BABY COLLECTION

Try cutting your rolled-out dough into the shape of baby vests, bibs or babygrows. These are almost the right size for tiny new arrivals. It is great fun adding slightly different details of poppers or collars to each one, and they are the perfect size for clearly writing the baby's name or date of birth.

If you know there is a much-loved toy in the family, such as a teddy or a rabbit, you could include this in your theme too.

Initials are also a good idea, or you could spell out the whole of the new baby's name in biscuits. Pretty pastel-coloured biscuits shaped like babies or churches can also make a lovely centrepiece for a christening tea party or lunch table.

TEA PARTIES, HEN NIGHTS AND OTHER OCCASIONS

A collection of butterflies, dragonflies, watering cans and umbrellas would make a lovely summery present for someone, or be perfect for a tea party in the garden. Decorated in fresh greens, whites and pinks and finished with summer flowers, these charming biscuits are sure to be appreciated.

For hen nights and girly parties, biscuits shaped like handbags, dresses and shoes are always a huge hit with girls of all ages. They can be as pretty, chic or contemporary as you like. You could also include a few shaped like cakes, cups and saucers and teapots to continue the tea party theme.

CHRISTMAS COLLECTION

Use the Gorgeous Gingerbread recipe on page 182 and cutters in festive shapes to make Christmas biscuits. I like the gingerbread iced simply with white royal icing. Packed into cellophane bags and tied with gingham or Christmas ribbon, these biscuits make very personal and different presents. They are also lovely personalised with Christmas messages or names, and are beautiful hung with ribbon on the Christmas tree (see page 110).

SAY IT WITH BISCUITS

Biscuits make fantastic presents, and putting a little effort into choosing a pretty way to wrap them or finding an unusual tin or container can turn them into a stunning gift. Here are a few ideas to inspire you.

Boxes

Gift boxes, cardboard boxes and chic transparent cubes are all great for turning biscuits into presents (a variety of these containers can be found on www.cakecraftshop.co.uk, www.squires-shop.com or www.cakescookiesandcraftshop.co.uk). If you want to put biscuits straight into a box, a piece of kitchen paper at the bottom will stop the biscuits from sliding around inside. They also look pretty wrapped in layers of tissue paper inside the box. Biscuits make a great present to send by post, but always make sure you wrap different types separately (to avoid them going soggy) and that they are tightly packed (bubble wrap is useful for this), otherwise they will knock into each other in transit.

Baking Tins

It's a fun idea to present biscuits in baking tins. For example, you could fill a vintage loaf tin with biscuits, then wrap it in cellophane or brown paper before tying with string or ribbon.

Gift bags

Cellophane bags (available from places such as Lakeland and Squires) look very attractive when tied with a pretty ribbon, and they also keep biscuits fresh and tasty. I like to keep an eye out for old-fashioned sweet shop bags and little fabric bags: the biscuits cannot be stored for long in them as they will soon go soggy or stale, but these wrappings do look nice.

Jars

Kilner jars or vintage jars are wonderful containers for biscuits, and make a thoughtful, quirky present to say you are thinking of someone. Collect them from jumble sales or junk shops, or buy new ones.

Say it with many...

It is lovely to give one type of biscuit as a present, but extra special to make a number of different types and pack up a selection box. It is important to wrap each type of biscuit separately before arranging them all in a tin, box or basket. I like to put in a little card to explain all the different types of biscuits I have included.

Biscuit kits

Instead of giving biscuits as a present why not encourage others to make their own? Simply weigh all the dry ingredients into a jar (it is usually better to leave out the butter and egg and let the recipient add them), attach a cutter and the recipe, and let the fun begin. This is a truly creative gift.

Tins

A tin full of biscuits makes a wonderful present and might also inspire the recipient to make more biscuits at a later date to fill the tin again.

A big thank you to...

My mum, who taught me to bake, and **my dad** for eating everything with gusto – for your unfailing support, encouragement and for being such wonderful grandparents, without which none of this would have been possible. **My mother-in-law Penny**, for being 'Granny Molly', for supporting me throughout the process and for being a constant source of inspiration as well as a wonderful cook and advisor on all things culinary. **My friends**, who have christened me the 'biscuit fairy' and their 'feeder' in moments of biscuit overload. Thank you for forgiving me for disappearing into the magical world of biscuits and for all your help, feedback and enthusiastic munching and for kindly sharing precious recipes. **Hollie**, a patient ear and motivator over many a 'cup of tea and a chat', and **Rosie**, for being a wonderful baking consultant. **Mary Berry**, for her encouragement, inspiration and support, and for believing in me both throughout *The Great British Bake Off* and subsequently. **Paul Hollywood**, for motivating me always to achieve my very best. **Mel and Sue**, for loving my baking and for stealing my ingredients. **Lucy Young**, for sharing her wealth of knowledge and encouraging me to achieve my ambitions. **Elly**, for her unwaveringly sound advice, friendship and uplifting spirit, for which I am enormously grateful. **Heather**, for her invaluable guidance, expertise and vision. **Imogen**, for guiding me through the world of books, for loving my ideas and for bringing them to life. And to the fantastic team at **Ebury** for all their support, commitment and enthusiasm. **James**, for creating such a stunning design. **Hannah**, for her wonderful Aga expertise. **Lucy**, for lending me her beautiful kitchen for the cover shots, and to **Mel** for her styling and expert guidance. **Laura**, **Katie** and **Polly** for making my biscuits look so lovely and helping to create the book. **Love Productions** and the **BBC**, for *The Great British Bake Off*, for giving me such a fantastic opportunity, and for inspiring me to make baking my life. **Chris** and **Anne** for helping to guide my path into the literary and media world.